INVESTIGATING THE NATURAL WORLD
OF CHEMISTRY WITH KIDS

D0620112

Arthur with a lighted taper
Touched the fire to Grandpa's paper
Grandpa leaped a foot or higher
Dropped the sheet and shouted "Fire!"
Arthur, wrapped in contemplation,
Viewed the scene of conflagration
"This" he said, "confirms my notion—
Heat creates both light and motion."

—*Beastly Boys and Ghastly Girls*, Wallace Irwin

Investigating the Natural World of Chemistry with Kids

Experiments, Writing, and Drawing Activities for Learning Science

Michael J. Strauss

with illustrations by Lynn Jeffery

Universal-Publishers
Boca Raton

Investigating the Natural World of Chemistry with Kids:
Experiments, Writing, and Drawing Activities for Learning Science

Universal-Publishers
Boca Raton, Florida, USA • 2012

ISBN-10: 1-61233-155-6/ ISBN-13: 978-1-61233-155-3

www.universal-publishers.com

Chapter opening illustrations copyright © 1995 by Lynn Jeffery

The first printing published in 1995 by Heinemann as *Where Puddles Go - Investigating Science with Kids* is referenced by name in the Introduction to this edition.

Excerpt from GENIUS: THE LIFE AND SCIENCE OF RICHARD PEYNMAN by James Gleick. Copyright © 1992. Reprinted by permission of Pantheon Books, a Division of Random House, Inc.

Dialogue for Chapter 1, "Evaporation," originally appeared in "Evaporation: A Constructivist Dialogue" by Michael J. Strauss in *Journal of Humanistic Education and Development* (vol. 32, 1994). Reprinted by permission of the Editor.

Dialogue for Chapter 5, "Mixing," originally appeared in "What's Pure?" by Michael J. Strauss in *ETC: A Review of General Semantics*. Copyright © 1994 by the International Society for General Semantics. Reprinted by permission of the Editor.

Publisher's Cataloging Information

Strauss, Michael J., 1940-
    Investigating the natural world of chemistry with kids : experiments, writing, and drawing activities for learning science / Michael J. Strauss; with illustrations by Lynn Jeffrey.
        p. cm.
    Includes index.
    Summary: Contains a variety of experiments that illustrate such basic principles of physical change as condensation, evaporation, melting and freezing, and crystallization.
    ISBN 978-1-61233-155-3 (pbk. : alk. paper) -- ISBN 1-61233-155-6 (pbk. : alk. paper)
    1. Physics—Experiments—Juvenile literature. 2. Physics projects—Juvenile literature.
[1. Physics—Experiments. 2. Experiments.] I. Jeffrey, Lynn, ill. II. Title.
    QC26.S77 1995
    536.4'0078—dc20   2012914594

To Merissa and Matthew,
who taught me by asking questions—
about bugs and bubbles and stones—
in the backyard, and down by
the river

Contents

Acknowledgments

Toby Fulwiler played a pivotal role in the beginning stages of this book and provided critical advice on the initial draft. As colleague, mentor, and friend over the past ten years, he has shown me many new ways to be a teacher and writer. I thank Richard Hazler, editor of the *Journal of Humanistic Education and Development*, and Jeremy Klein, editor of *ETC: A Review of General Semantics*, for their enthusiastic response to two of the dialogues which were first submitted to their journals and subsequently published there. I am grateful to Gregory Bateson for his dialogues, which also first appeared in *ETC:* and in other journals in the 1950s, and subsequently as *Metalogues* in his book *Steps to an Ecology of Mind.* They provided the dialogue form I have used. Though I never met or heard him in person, his books *Mind and Nature* and *Steps*, have played a significant role in my thoughts about science and about science teaching.

I am grateful also to the hundreds of children and teachers I have met at Vermont's elementary schools, museums, and libraries who welcomed me into their classrooms and reading rooms, and shared their excitement about science with me as we did experiments and talked with each other.

I thank my colleagues Bill Biddle and Tony Magistrale for constant encouragement, and Leigh Peake, my editor at Heinemann, who has worked with me—week to week—via fax, phone, and letter, to help fashion the final manuscript. Without her constant encouragement and critical but supportive feedback, the book would never have been completed. I appreciate the final technical review by my friend and colleague, Willem Leenstra, and for the support of my writing group, Corinne Glesne, Glenda Bissex, Laura Fulwiler, and Toby Fulwiler.

Preface

I recall that as a youngster of about eleven I got out of bed one summer evening around 1:00 A.M. and very quietly crept outside to climb up on the roof of our house. On my back watching for meteorites I waited next to my box camera, which I had set up with an open shutter, pointing skyward. About three hours later, clicking the shutter closed in the dark, I carefully returned to my room. It was an experiment I'd read about in a science magazine. The developed picture, with its short arc of streaking starlight and meteoric light lines, was my first personal knowledge that the earth really did rotate. Of course I knew this from school, from books, and from watching the sun rise and set. But my real gut feeling was of a stationary earth, and of the sun moving up and down. That picture really made the earth rotate for me. Well, it wasn't really the picture. It was the experience of taking the picture. Of being out on the roof watching while the film absorbed starlight.

The picture long ago crumbled away. I remember showing it to friends, who really weren't impressed at all. But the experience of taking it is still with me. It was part of my path towards a life in science, a rather convoluted path, with many dead ends, bungled experiments, and more than a few explosions that have left me a bit deaf in my left ear. I learned a lot in school, but my love of science really came from playing out in back lots, building things in our garage, mixing up concoctions in the toolshed, and making rockets out of old seltzer cartridges and powdered match heads (a very hazardous and risky business). Curiosity, experimenting, and constant wondering were the keys to all of this. They are still with me as I write, teach, and do experiments with young people to create the kind of excitement that makes science fun.

My experience of science in school wasn't the same as my own free experimentation outside of the classroom. It was more structured, organized, and prescriptive, and I was constantly evaluated about how much I knew. Still, it was my favorite subject. But I have come to believe that the motivating force for a lifetime in science—or any subject—often comes not only from school, but from a deeply imbedded curiosity about how the world works. Learning about science needs to be active, collaborative, and connected to the everyday personal lives of children. During the last few years the National Science Foundation (NSF) has increased funding for programs that are trying to do exactly this, both inside and outside of school. This book is an outgrowth of that effort, a direct result of NSF funding to promote a constructivist approach to the teaching and learning of science.

The term "constructivist" is popular, educational shoptalk these days, but I use it here reluctantly. You won't find it in Webster's *New Encyclopedic Dictionary*. I know, because after writing it down in a draft of the Preface, I tried looking it up. It isn't really complicated. It's what I was doing up on the roof with my camera late that summer night. I was constructing a personal view of the world and how it works. *Where Puddles Go* was written with the hope that some of your children might become fascinated with the dialogues, experiments, and questions here, like I was with the magazine article that prompted my rooftop journey. Even more importantly, it was written to help you and your children have a good time together, beginning an exploration of the science of chemistry. Enjoy!

Introduction

For Parents and Teachers

About Change

Children constantly wonder about the natural world and ask all kinds of questions. Where do puddles go? How do clouds form? Where does frost come from? And snow? It's natural for them to wonder because everything is always appearing, disappearing, or turning into something else. Water falls from clouds as rain on one day, and the next day the sky is clear and the water is gone. Flowers, trees, and people grow, and then get old and die. Everything is always changing. Sometimes change is rapid, like when leaves burn in a fire. Sometimes it's very slow, like when flowers grow in a garden.

This is a book about the nature of change, for parents, teachers, and children. It's a collection of humorous conversations, pictures, and activities designed to help children understand how and why changes happen in the world. It does this by helping them imagine the movement and arrangement of the very smallest parts of things: atoms and molecules.

If all scientific knowledge were lost in a single cataclysm, what single statement would preserve the most information for following generations? The famous physicist Richard Feynman answered as follows:

> All things are made of atoms—little particles that move around in perpetual motion, attracting each other when they are a little distance apart, but repelling when squeezed into one another. In that one sentence, you will see, there is an enormous amount of information about the world, if just a little imagination and thinking are applied.

Where Puddles Go was created to help you and your children apply a little imagination and thinking to the very simple idea of atoms, the little particles that move about and make up the world.

A World of Changing Parts

The world is composed of parts, some quite large and some very small. On a clear night you can see stars shine as separate points of light in the sky. The ocean beach is a very large collection of separate grains of sand. Rain comes in many single drops and cookies break into crumbs. Just about everything can come apart into separate chunks, bits, or pieces. In this book you will read, write, draw, talk, and experiment with children about how the very smallest parts of things arrange themselves in various forms.

So imagine a tiny bit of something: a piece of dust, a crumb, or a tiny speck of sand. Ask your children: "What would happen if you broke it up into even smaller pieces, and then broke one of these smaller pieces into even smaller pieces? What if you kept on doing this over and over again? What would the very smallest piece be like?" Because it's so small it would be light, so light it would float. If a large number of these pieces were all together in a pile you could see them, but if they were far apart from each other you couldn't. They can't be seen, even with a very powerful microscope. All you see is the empty space between the pieces. The "stuff" itself would be invisible. Our eyes cannot see the very smallest parts of things!

One way children can learn about change is to see how the very smallest parts of things fit together, and how they alter their position from one moment to the next. In a movie or on television, showing movement is easy. As the pictures appear on the screen one after another you see them connected together over time and the objects move. The fact that we are seeing a series of still images in sequence escapes conscious awareness; what becomes apparent is movement or change. In *Where Puddles Go,* we will show separate pictures at different times so children can understand how the smallest parts of things can come together and be visible, like a puddle, and then drift apart to become invisible.

Things in the world are large collections of very small bits—the atoms—in different patterns or forms. Different things, as well as changes in the world—forming clouds, falling rain, or growing flowers—all result from the movement of these very small bits from one pattern to another. Understanding simple physical change, the topic of the first eight chapters of *Where Puddles Go,* is the very beginning, the bedrock, of learning about more complex chemical changes that result in the exquisite forms and patterns of the natural world. The last chapter, 9, *Making Something New,* is an introduction to simple chemical change.

Using this Book

Personal and "Secondhand" Knowledge

The largest part of this book is a set of imaginary dialogues about change. The dialogues were assembled during the past five years, from fragments of many conversations with elementary school children, as part of a National Science Foundation program for Teacher Enhancement in Physical Science. They focus on the difference between personal knowledge or experience, and knowledge obtained "secondhand" from a teacher or text. Gregory Bateson used a similar dialogue form in his book, *Steps to an Ecology of Mind* (Bateson, Gregory. 1972. New York, N.Y.: Random House).

The use of human interaction and dialogue in the teaching and learning of science is consistent with what we know about the role of language in learning. It has been known for some time that children learn and understand new information better when they use their own language to express connections between that new information (observations and experiences) and what they have already come to believe.

The dialogues in *Where Puddles Go* focus exactly on this issue. They are concerned with how children create meaning when they are confronted with secondhand knowledge of "non-sensed" objects and abstract definitions and terms. Reading other peoples' definitions in a book, or being told about someone else's ideas (especially about small invisible particles) is secondhand knowledge. It's not personal and it doesn't come from direct experience. The smallest parts of things are invisible, and "not sensed" often does mean *non-sense*, especially to a child who operates in the world of concrete things which can be seen, touched, and heard. Under such circumstances, children often just memorize the ideas and words of others, and then try to combine them with personal life experiences in an attempt to create meaning. But this meaning often is far from the commonly accepted scientific view of the world.

Children often have already established misconceptions and misunderstandings about many phenomena. The teacher's and parent's task is not only to discover what those naive explanations are, but to enable students to change and replace them. The dialogues model this process of discovery and learning.

Many years ago, before views of the earth from the space shuttle and the moon were common in magazines, books, television, and film, a teacher once asked a group of young children, "How many of you know the earth is round?" All the children in the class raised their hands. They all knew the "right" answer. They had been told, and the fact was in their textbooks. While their hands were still all raised, the teacher asked, "How many of you really believe it?" Most of the hands came down. The fact of a round earth was not personal knowledge. Their experience was of a flat or bumpy earth. A round earth was teacher or textbook knowledge, perhaps not to be trusted in one's personal life, but good for the classroom and for examinations. The children made a clear distinction between their personal knowledge of the world—what they really believed—and a separate kind of "secondhand" knowledge, as obtained from a teacher or text.

Active Learning, Engagement, and Familiar Language

Where Puddles Go will help you help your children make more meaningful connections between their own world and the world of atoms and molecules. The focus is on personal experience and how models are developed, how one can reason about the world, and how knowledge about it is constructed. Children are encouraged to become active rather than passive learners: To discover meaning in their own world, not just in the ideas or definitions of others.

The methods are more involved than a simple presentation of facts. Children often expect to receive preformed *factual* knowledge. That kind of teaching is where the teacher *fills* the students with *deposits* of information. Students are required to store them for future use, even though the connections between parts, as well as any personal meaning associated with them, is missing. Students are not required to really know, but to memorize. The content about which they are supposed to think is the property of the teacher.

Because of this, children's enthusiasm for science often diminishes as they approach middle school. Science becomes less spontaneous and more work. What happens? The content gets larger and more formal, and children's experience of it becomes less direct. It is less about personal experience and more about others' ideas, thoughts, and terms, many of which don't seem to make sense. Abstraction creeps in. And young people are constantly judged about their knowledge of those abstract ideas, thoughts, and terms.

This doesn't have to happen. Engaging children in active learning often takes more time, may lead in unforeseen directions, and sometimes can generate more questions than answers. Nevertheless, knowledge constructed in this way is more profound and long-lasting. *Where Puddles Go* is designed to help you integrate the ideas and terms of science into children's personal lives using familiar language. Exploration and inquiry begin first in order to provide a grounding for more abstract concepts and ideas that follow. Learning always begins with engagement prior to the introduction of new terminology or concepts. The focus of each introductory discussion and dialogue (see *Getting Started* in each chapter) is precisely this—engagement—followed by direct connections to personal experiences and observations in the experiments that follow.

The Role of Parents and Teachers

Your role as teacher or parent is to be an observer, facilitator, and guide, focusing children and posing questions that lead away from dead ends and toward understanding. With lots of dialogue, discussion, and experiments, the arrangement and movement of atoms and molecules can develop into an explanatory principle with real, personal meaning. If children then talk and share with each other what they know and what they don't, and then come to a common understanding, the leap from the concrete "see touch" world to the world of abstraction is made easier. Writing and drawing exercises, as well as more experiments, provide additional steps where meaning and understanding can be revised and consolidated.

Where Puddles Go deals with the science of chemistry, proceeding from simple concepts like evaporation to more complex concepts like chemical reactions. This contrasts with many science activity books that are a hodgepodge of hundreds of unrelated activities with no general principles or underlying focus. The chapters in *Where Puddles Go* can be done as individual, unrelated units or in sequence, from Chapter 1 through 9. The latter is preferred. Understanding condensation is much easier if you first understand evaporation, and so on. As children proceed from chapter to chapter, they will become more at ease and familiar with careful observation, questioning, experimenting, and drawing conclusions. Topics are partly open-ended, though suggestions and ideas for experiments and activities are plentiful. The dialogues and activities lend themselves to cooperative group work where children compare ideas, drawings, writing, and feelings about what they have seen and done.

Parts of the Book

Each chapter in *Where Puddles Go* is devoted to a specific kind of change. Chapters 1 through 8 are about physical changes such as melting, freezing, and boiling. All chapters (except Chapter 9) are divided into five sections: Dialogue; Description and Pictures; Experiments; Questions to Write and Draw; For Parents and Teachers.

Dialogues

The Dialogues are between parents and children. The children all know each other. They are either brothers and sisters, or neighbors. They are asking questions about everyday phenomena like puddles disappearing, ice melting, or sugar dissolving, which all children have experienced. The dialogues focus on ways of explaining these in terms of changes in the underlying, submicroscopic structure of water, ice, and sugar. Technical and more abstract terms like *atoms, molecules,* and *kinetic energy* are not used extensively. The dialogues may be read to younger children as stories, followed by discussion, questions, and further elaboration by the teacher or parent. Older children might take a more active role, reading or acting out the dialogues themselves.

All the dialogues model children hypothesizing and asking questions about what they observe in their own lives. With parents as facilitators and guides, they promote a personal understanding of change in terms of the movement and arrangement of very small parts, the atoms and molecules that compose substance.

Descriptions

The Descriptions are a written version of the Picture. A Description explains the change in simple, nontechnical language. Scientific terms are not used extensively, and analogies and metaphors are provided where they are appropriate. The pictorial and written versions of the phenomena reinforce each other, providing visual and discursive representations of the concept. You may wish to have children write or elaborate the particular change in their own language using the verbal description and pictures as a guide.

Pictures

The Pictures graphically represent the phenomena in each dialogue and follow the Description. They provide a concrete referent for the abstract concept of small, invisible parts of things. Each picture shows how the position, movement, and arrangement of small parts results in visible structure and change. The bits are collected in different arrangements, close together and far apart, over time. The animation and characters allow children to personally identify with the structure and process in question, supporting the theme of the dialogue.

Children may wish to recast these pictures in their own way by drawing personal visions of small parts constructing a whole. The idea of invisible small bits comprising a visible object or substance is reinforced by this effort. You may wish to purchase some small Styrofoam® spheres or marbles which will allow them to model the structure and change in question. A group of children can role-play the bits themselves, moving far apart around the room and close together in a tightly packed group.

A Word About Images   The cartoons in *Where Puddles Go* are humorous and lighthearted, and meant to convey that chemistry is more about everyday life than about laboratories, test tubes, and people in white lab coats. It occurs in the kitchen, on the playground, in the garden, and at the beach. So the cartoons reflect the excitement and wonder of science in the lives of children. This is in contrast to the sterile and impersonal image many children (and adults) have about science and scientists, a view fostered by images on television and in movies. (The evil, faceless scientists in Steven Spielberg's extremely popular *E.T.* come immediately to mind.) Most scientists really aren't like that.

Experiments

The Experiments provide children with direct experience of the change in question. Such experience is critical to a meaningful understanding of the phenomena. They are prompted to carefully observe, question, and hypothesize in order to create ideas in their own language which explain the phenomena.

Questions to Write and Draw

The Questions to Write and Draw extend and amplify the experiments, prompting more thought and questions about what children have observed and read in the dialogue.

Writing to Learn Science   It is critically important for you to use and adapt *Where Puddles Go* for the level of cognitive development of the children you are working with. However, it is assumed they will have begun the process of writing and/or drawing, for the book relies heavily on the Chinese proverb: *I hear, I forget; I see, I remember; I do, I understand.* The last phrase might also be *I write (or draw), I understand,* for children learn the most by thinking about what they are doing. And one of the best ways of thinking is writing, meaning writing *Writ Large.* This includes drawing pictures, making diagrams, writing numbers, and making lists, as well as writing sentences and paragraphs. Putting thoughts on a page, in either words or pictures, takes them out of children's heads before they vanish and places them in front of their eyes so they can see what they understand and what they don't. And then rewriting and redrawing—a revision of thought—can occur. This is the very essence of learning!

For Parents and Teachers

Getting Started   The *Getting Started* section is for the teacher or parent. It has suggestions for getting children to start thinking about the topic and relating it to their own lives. The suggestions are quite specific, but are only some of many possible ways in which each topic can be introduced. It may be beneficial to write down children's comments and observations in a journal.

A Deeper Look   A Deeper Look is also for the teacher or parent. Highly motivated, older, or more advanced students may also be interested in this section, which is a more technical and detailed description of the subject. While brief, it is similar in content to basic material from introductory middle and high school chemistry texts, but sufficiently comprehensive so that those needn't be consulted. Some of the material in this section repeats that in the Descriptions for younger children, but at a much higher level and with more technical terms. The redundancy is purposeful. Students who understand the simple description have the option of reading a more technical version later on. Technical topics covered in the Deeper Look section of each chapter are listed below.

Chapter 1. Where Puddles Go

Size of atoms and molecules
Numbers of atoms and molecules
Attractive forces between molecules
Movement of molecules
Molecular structure of liquids
Molecular structure of gases
Evaporation—changing from a liquid to a gas
Heat and molecular motion

Chapter 2. Where Drops Come From

Properties of gases
Behavior of molecules in a gas
Kinetic energy and motion of molecules
Changes of state
Condensation—changing from a gas to a liquid
Steam and water vapor
Humidity
Clouds
Rain

Chapter 3. Disappearing in the Drink

Molecules, atoms, and ions in solids
Ionic solids, molecular solids
Crystals—sugar and salt
Dissolving a solid in a liquid
Solute, solvent, and solutions
Solutions of gases in liquids

Chapter 4. Appearing in the Drink

Crystallization
Difference between freezing and crystallization from
    solution
Dissolving in and crystallizing from water
Ions and molecules in solution
Effect of temperature and concentration on solubility
Crystallization from evaporating aqueous solutions
Types of crystals
Crystals from ions and crystals from molecules
Seeding to help crystallization
Crystal forms

Chapter 5. Putting Things Together

Elements and compounds
Symbols for elements
Periodic table of the elements
Nature of compounds
Differences between elements and compounds
Introduction to formulas
Introduction to chemical combination
Types of mixtures—element/element; compound/
    compound; element/compound
Mixture of states—solid/liquid; gas/liquid; gas/gas
Homogeneous and heterogeneous mixtures
Overview of pure substances and mixtures

Chapter 6. Taking Things Apart

Ways of separating mixtures
Separating heterogeneous mixtures

Separating by hand (solid from a solid)
Separating by filtration (insoluble solid from a liquid)
Separation of homogeneous mixtures
Separation by evaporation (soluble solid from a liquid)
Heterogeneous liquid mixtures
The separatory funnel
Distillation
Chromatography

Chapter 7. Getting In and Out of Shape

The nature of heat
The nature of temperature
Kinetic energy—energy of motion
Centigrade and Fahrenheit temperature
Motion and heat; motion and temperature
Intensive and extensive properties
Changes of state again
Melting and freezing
Warming a solid
Melting a solid
Direction of heat flow
Decomposition and melting

Chapter 8. Making Bubbles

Heating substances again
Changing the phase of a substance again
Melting and boiling points of substances
Temperature and change of state
Heat and change of state
Molecular changes during vaporization
Formation of bubbles throughout the liquid phase
Invisible vapor vs. visible liquid
General description of vaporization
Sublimation

Chapter 9. Making Something New

Chemical change vs. physical change
Forming compounds from elements
Representation of chemical change
Chemical symbols reviewed
Formulas and formula units
The chemical equation
Signs and symbols in equations

Where Puddles Go is most appropriate and adaptable for children between the ages of five and twelve years. Younger children might have more difficulty with the later chapters (7–9), but the activities and level can be simplified and shortened to fashion a program of learning appropriate for each child. Even older students in their sophomore, junior, and senior years in high school may find the section labeled A Deeper Look a useful introduction to some topics in chemistry. The book is written in a way to encourage parents, teachers, and children to work together, ask questions, and explore the nature of physical change. In terms of cognitive development, parents and teachers are in the best position to build on the early excitement and curiosity children have about science to help make it last a lifetime.

Most of the activities in *Where Puddles Go* require no special equipment or materials. Much of the focus is on the kitchen where a lot of fascinating chemistry occurs every day at mealtime and snack time. The supplies are, for the most part, in the kitchen cabinet, grocery store, hardware store, or drugstore. You might want to reserve a cabinet in the kitchen or shelves at school for all the materials you will use (dishes, glasses, paper, pencils, sugar, salt . . .). The book is appropriate for use in both the classroom and at home, and teachers may wish to give parents a copy for use outside of school.

We Are All Scientists

When you enter a dark house at night, you switch on a lamp near the front door. If it doesn't go on, your first thought will probably be that the bulb has burned out. You switch on the wall light, which does go on. There is a spare bulb in the drawer of the table right beneath the lamp, so you replace the bulb, but the lamp still doesn't go on. So the absence of power to the lamp is probably due to something else.

Since the wall light went on in the same room as the lamp, you've ruled out the circuit breaker which controls that portion of your home, and your attention now focuses directly on the lamp in question. With the lamp switch set to ON, you move the cord on the lamp a bit and the lamp goes on. You move it again and the lamp goes off. By moving the cord back and forth, you cause the light to go on and off. Your conclusion: There is a loose connection where the cord connects to the lamp.

You've answered the question: "Why didn't the light go on when I flipped the switch?" by using the scientific method to find out, and to solve your problem. It's almost a spontaneous process in this simple example. You don't say to yourself, "I'm going to use the scientific method to solve this problem," and then start thinking about hypotheses, experiments, observations, and conclusions; you just do it. Life has taught you how. There are other reasons why the light might not have worked (a defective socket, a broken switch, a broken plug). Your method eliminated all but one. If jiggling the cord didn't work, you would have had to probe further, checking the plug, the switch, etc. The whole process can be broken down in the following way:

Observation: The lamp doesn't light

Hypothesis: If a circuit breaker for the room has switched off, the lamp won't go on

Experiment: Try another light in the room, which won't go on if circuit breaker has switched off

Results: Other light in the room goes on

Conclusion: Circuit breaker has *not* switched off

Hypothesis: If bulb is burned out the lamp won't go on

Experiment: Replace lamp bulb with a new bulb

Results: Lamp still doesn't go on

Conclusion: Bulb is *not* burned out

Hypothesis: If there is a loose connection in the cord to the lamp the light won't go on

Experiment: Jiggle the cord to see if connection can be made

Results: Light goes on and off as cord is moved back and forth

Conclusion: There *is* a loose connection from the cord to the lamp

This repeating sequence of *hypothesis, experiment, results,* and *conclusion* illustrates, in a very simple fashion, a scientific approach to problem solving. And you probably can see that it is how many of us, including children, solve problems. Often you do it very rapidly and spontaneously. You have a large backlog of personal experience and knowledge which allows you to do it so fast. When the light doesn't go on, you don't presume the reason was a full moon or a black cat that crossed your path as you approached the house. You associate light bulbs with electricity, power companies, circuit breakers, power cords, and light switches, not with the moon or black cats. (However, if you wanted to you could check moon and black cat hypotheses to rule them out.)

Though their backlog of personal experience is smaller, children initiate just this sort of problem solving. Something as simple as stacking blocks may involve a simpler but unarticulated sequence: A *hypothesis* (thinking) about how to stack them so they don't fall over, *experiments* (trial and error) in block stacking, *results* by seeing which stacks fall and which don't, and a *conclusion* about which block stacking method works best. Throwing balls through hoops, building with Legos®, and learning to ride a bicycle all involve similar kinds of processes, though not necessarily articulated in language. It's one way of living, interacting, and learning about the world—a form of play. In *Where Puddles Go,* you and your children will be doing exactly this: Making observations; hypothesizing explanations; doing experiments; and drawing conclusions.

Where Puddles Go was written so you and your children can have a good time learning some serious chemistry. Let's begin!

Where Puddles Go

Evaporating

> *They say the cause of perfume disappearing is evaporation. Evaporation gets blamed for many things people forget to put the top on.*

Diana: Daddy, where do puddles go?

Father: Puddles, my dear, simply go and form new puddles somewhere else.

D: But that's silly, Daddy. Puddles just get smaller, and then they disappear.

F: Are you sure? Have you ever seen that happen?

D: Yes, Daddy, I have. When I left for school this morning there was a little puddle in the driveway right next to my bicycle and when I got home it was just a tiny puddle. And now at dinner time it's gone. It disappeared. Where did it go?

F: Did you see it vanish?

D: Not all at once I didn't! It takes a long time. I can't see the hands on my watch change, either, but they do. It was three o'clock when I came home and now my watch says six. It's the same with grass and flowers. I know they grow, but I can't see them do it.

F: Tell me, are the hands on your watch, and the grass and flowers, like puddles?

D: Well, . . . no. They don't disappear like the puddle. And what I really want to know is where the puddle goes. Where does it go to, Daddy? Do you know? Tell me where it goes.

F: It's just like the hands on your watch, dear. The puddle goes to a different place, like the hands move to a different position on your watch dial.

D: But where? *Show me where it went to!* It's not on the street or anywhere else near here. In fact all the puddles on our block have disappeared. They're all gone. Where did they go to?

F: Maybe they went to China, or Alaska, or the North Pole.

D: How could they get to China or Alaska? How would they get there? How come I can't see them fly away?

F: Now that's an interesting question. How do you know they fly? When you're not looking at the puddle maybe little pieces of it just slide along the ground to Alaska? They could sneak away when you're in school and take the interstate up to the border and. . . .

D: Daddy, stop it!! You're teasing me. Puddle pieces don't slide on the ground. That's stupid. I don't care where they go if you won't tell me.

F: OK, OK. Then let's get back to that "flying" idea. Where did you get the idea that puddles fly.

D: Well, I've never seen a puddle fly either. But the driveway is so hard. Puddles can't go down through it like water goes into the dirt in my flower pot when I water my flowers. The puddle on the driveway just seems to get smaller and smaller and then . . . it's just gone! And I don't really understand where it goes. If it flew away wouldn't I see pieces of it lift up in the air when it leaves for somewhere else?

F: I wonder if you would see pieces of puddle if they lifted up in the air? Can you see things lift up into the air?

D: Yes! I see airplanes lift up, and birds, and balloons and leaves when the wind blows, and smoke too.

F: But not puddles?

D: No, not puddles. Puddles don't fly or lift up. They just sit on the ground and disappear.

F: It's just like when you hang up your bathing suit to dry. The water in the wet suit goes to the same place that puddle water goes to!

D: OK, let's go eat. Mommy is making fried chicken! You can tell me where puddles go later.

F: Hey, wait a second. How do you know Mommy's making fried chicken?

D: Because I can *smell* it. Can't you smell it? Let's go eat.

F: So you can't see it from here, but you know it's there because you can smell it.

D: Yes.

F: And how do you do that?

D: With my nose of course, like everyone else!

F: And how, my dear, does the chicken get into your nose?

D: Oh, Daddy, stop it. The chicken doesn't get into my nose. The smell of the chicken gets into my nose.

F: Oh, of course. Well, what *is* the smell, and how does it get from the fried chicken in the kitchen to your nose here on the front porch?

D: I guess it comes through the air. Is that right, Daddy? Does it come through the air?

F: Yes, I think it must. It's the same thing, you know—puddles disappearing and your smelling the chicken.

D: It is? How is my smelling chicken the same as a puddle disappearing?

F: We would have to know what the smell *is* first.

D: It's nice and it makes me hungry. I like it . . ., let's eat. *Now!*

F: I wonder what it's made of.

D: I don't know, Daddy. You tell me. Maybe if we *tasted* it we could figure it out a lot easier!

F: I think a smell is like a puddle that has disappeared.

D: But that doesn't help at all. It doesn't tell me about where puddles go or what smells are. Let's go to dinner.

F: Imagine a small part of the fried chicken, so small that you can't see it, and very, very light—lighter than a speck of dust and smaller than a germ—floating off of the chicken into the air and traveling to your nose.

D: You mean a tiny piece of chicken skin? Or a bit of crust or some of the fried chicken seasoning powder that Mommy uses?

F: Much smaller than that. So small you can't see it. So light it floats in the air. Many, many millions of times smaller than a piece of dust or even a germ.

D: But I can smell it? Imagine that. Chicken dust, but much smaller!

F: Well, not really chicken dust, but yes, you can smell it. Human beings have very sensitive noses, you know.

D: I know, Daddy, because sometimes I can smell Mommy's chicken from next door at Danny's house.

F: Tiny bits of a puddle can also float up in the air because they're so light they hardly weigh anything at all. And if bits of puddle keep doing that over and over again all day long, then eventually the whole puddle will have risen up in the air, bit by bit, and will be gone. When the bits are all together on the ground in the puddle, it's easy to see them. But when they float away and are far apart you can't see them.

D: But where do all the tiny bits go?

F: Well, eventually they make clouds.

D: Clouds are made of water then.

F: They are.

D: Oh, I see, Daddy, I see. And then it rains and puddles form again somewhere else. Am I right?

F: Yes, dear, you are right.

D: Oh, Daddy, I think I knew that all along. Daddy?

F: What?

D: Why can I smell the chicken bits but not the puddle bits? Why is that, Daddy? And why don't the chicken bits rain down as fried chicken somewhere else?

F: Tomorrow, sweetie, tomorrow.

D: Daddy?

F: Yes.

D: Why do clouds look different than puddles? And why do they rain?

F: Tomorrow, sweetie.

Evaporating–A Description

Liquids are composed of a large number of very small bits, loosely attracted together. They move around but remain attached, as if they were holding hands. A group of people can hold hands but still move around can't they? They can't move as far as when they let go, however. A single bit is invisible because it is so small, but when a large number are all together the collection is visible, even though you can't see the individual bits themselves. A puddle of water is like this. Look at the picture of the puddle.

The bits move from place to place in the collection, some more rapidly than others. You could think of them as switching hands with each other, letting go for a short time to change position. Because of this *the liquid is fluid;*

24

it takes the shape of the bottom of the container it is in. The top is usually flat. As an example, think of a glass of water. If you pour the water into a glass of a different shape, the water will take that new shape, and it is always flat on top.

In a liquid some bits are moving fast and some are moving slower. They are constantly banging into each other. Bits near the surface which are moving relatively fast, can escape. There are no other bits on top of them, so if they are moving towards the surface, they don't bang into any other bits. They can just let go of the bits below and jump into the air above the liquid. When they do, *they are called a vapor.* The vapor is just a smaller number of bits floating in the air above the liquid. These have much larger spaces between them than when they are in the liquid form. Bits in the vapor do not hold hands because they are too far apart from each other. The vapor is invisible because the bits are so small and so far apart from each other. If the liquid is not covered with a lid or cap, water bits will keep escaping into the air until the liquid changes completely to a vapor. Water losing bits in this way is *evaporating.* It seems to disappear, but its bits just float up into the air and become an invisible vapor.

Heat makes the bits move. The hotter the liquid the faster they go and the less they hold hands. On a hot day bits will move faster and will thus escape more rapidly than they will on a cold day. Eventually, however, all the liquid will change into vapor; it will have evaporated and we can no longer see it. Remember, in a liquid there are many bits and they are quite close together so we can see them. In the vapor, bits are far apart and we cannot see them. Thus, when a liquid evaporates it seems to disappear.

In this description we used the phrase "holding hands" to explain a weak *attraction* of one small bit for another. Of course these bits really don't have hands to hold. It is just a visual way of describing how bits are attracted to each other. In further chapters which follow, this phrase is not used, but you may think of a weak attraction between bits in this way if it helps you understand how they behave. One kind of attraction you are familiar with is between a magnet and a piece of iron, like a small nail. You can feel this attraction if you hold the nail in one hand and the magnet in the other. While the attraction between the bits in water is not magnetic, it is similar to the *pull* you feel between the magnet and nail.

Evaporating

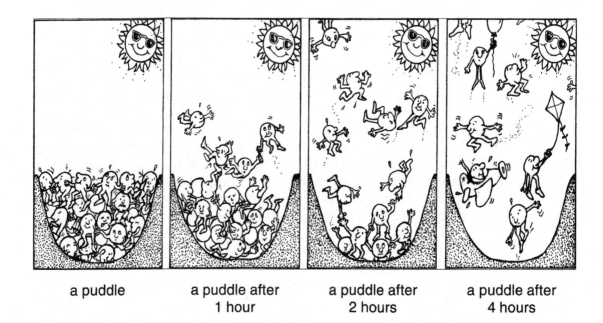

| a puddle | a puddle after 1 hour | a puddle after 2 hours | a puddle after 4 hours |

Experiments

YOU WILL NEED:
plates (1 white, 1 dark)
glass
salt
vegetable oil
water

 Pour a small puddle of water in two different plates. Put them in the hot sun. Cover one puddle with an upside-down glass. Keep a record of the size of each puddle at various times during the day.

 Which puddle disappears faster? Why? Draw two pictures of what happens. In the first, just draw what you see. In the second, show the water as small bits.

 Make two puddles of water on a hot sunny day, one on a white plate and one on a darker colored plate. Keep a record of the size of each puddle as time passes during the day. Which puddle disappears faster? Why? Should the puddles be the same size to start? Why or why not?

Make a puddle of vegetable oil and a puddle of water on two different plates in the hot sun. Keep a record of the size of each during the day. What do you observe? Can you explain your observations?

 Put a glass of water outside and keep a record of how full it is each day of the week. Make sure it doesn't rain in your glass. What happens?

 Make some salt water by mixing a lot of salt in a glass of water. Mix it until all the salt dissolves. Make a small puddle on a plate with some of this salt water and put it in the hot sun. Compare it with a similar sized puddle of regular water in the sun. After a full day is there any difference? After three days? Describe what you see. Draw a picture of what you see.

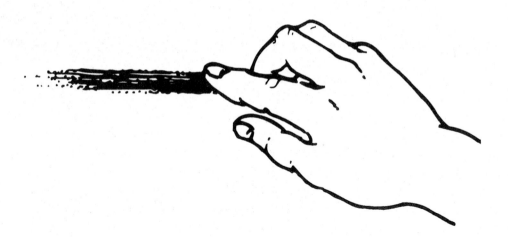

 Wet your finger and smear a thin film of water on a small blackboard or other similar surface. How long does it take to evaporate? Why do you think it evaporates faster than a puddle evaporates?

Questions to Write and Draw

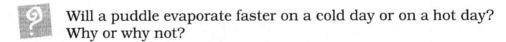

Will a puddle evaporate faster on a cold day or on a hot day? Why or why not?

Show how water vapor is different than liquid water. Draw a picture to illustrate your answer.

Where do you think water goes when a puddle evaporates? Could you write a letter to a friend explaining where it goes?

How do you think puddles form when it rains?

What is the opposite of evaporation? Describe it?

Will a covered glass of water evaporate? Why or why not? Would it evaporate if you put a hole in the cover?

Would a bigger hole result in faster evaporation than a small hole? Why or why not? Can you draw a picture to illustrate your answer?

Which will evaporate faster in the hot sun, a cup of water or the same amount of water poured onto a large dinner plate? Why?

If you pour vegetable oil on top of water in a glass, would the water evaporate as rapidly as it would without the oil? Why or why not? Could you design an experiment to find out? If you think you can, write down the details of the experiment before you do it.

If you put a solution of salt water in the sun, why doesn't the salt evaporate along with the water?

29

 When water evaporates it absorbs heat as it changes from liquid to vapor. When you get out of a hot bath with a thin layer of water on your body, do you notice this? What do you notice? How do you feel when you get out of a swimming pool and the wind is blowing? Does the wind help a thin film of water evaporate?

For Parents and Teachers

Getting Started

To get children interested and talking about evaporation, a small puddle of water can be poured out on a desk or the floor. Pose the question: "How can we get rid of this puddle?" Ask for suggestions and list them on a blackboard, overhead projector, or piece of paper. The suggestions will contain a variety of choices such as: "Wipe it up with a paper towel, push it off the edge of the desk into a pan, soak it up with newspapers, use a sponge, dry it up with a hair dryer, etc."

Ask about their own knowledge of puddles on the street or playground. Most children know that puddles get smaller and disappear when left alone. It's part of their everyday experience. If someone suggests leaving the puddle for a few days you can focus on that. If they don't, ask: "What would happen if I leave it there for a few days? Will it disappear?"

Pose the question: "Where do puddles go to when they disappear?" Write down a list of responses again. Focus on those closest to the explanation elaborated in the dialogue and description of evaporation in the previous section of this chapter.

A Deeper Look

Water is composed of small bits called water *molecules.* They are the smallest possible part of water. Visible water is a large collection of an extremely large number of water molecules. Such a large collection can exist in three different forms or *phases: solid* (ice), *liquid* (the colloquial use of the name water is the same as this phase), and *gas* (an invisible vapor). Most consumable liquids (foods) are water-based, like soda, milk, juice, tea, etc. Water-based liquids are called *aqueous.* These are discussed in more detail in Chapter 3. There are many nonaqueous liquids as well, such as oil, gasoline, and turpentine. However, except for the vegetable oils, these are often poisonous. Each is composed of different molecules (oil molecules, gasoline molecules, and turpentine molecules). For experiments with a nonaqueous liquid you should only use vegetable oil. Most others are too hazardous. Many aqueous liquids are hazardous as well (for example, ammonia and bleach), so think carefully about what you decide to use if you extend the experiments described.

A single molecule is invisible because it's so small. In the children's description molecules are called "bits" to express the idea in language and terminology close to their personal experience of "bits" of things. They have all experienced bits of dust, sand, sugar, and salt. However, molecules are much smaller than a normal "bit" of dust or salt. Extremely large numbers of molecules collected together can be seen as a visible amount of substance. That extremely large number is too big to adequately represent to children in normal number form. In a teaspoon of water it approaches the number of grains of sand on a very large stretch of ocean beach! You might use this visual representation to express how small a water molecule really is! Using large numbers with lots of zeros (i.e., 1,000,000,000,000,000,000,000,000 water molecules in a large spoon full of water) is less effective unless children understand the meaning of all those zeros. To be precise, there are about 6×10^{23} molecules in 18 grams of water (a six followed by twenty-three zeros).

In the diagrams of evaporation, the size of water molecules relative to the size of the puddle are greatly exaggerated. In addition, the number of molecules in the diagram of the puddle is much smaller than the number of molecules in a real puddle. You should be aware of this when you talk with children about these pictures, and for older children you may wish to mention it explicitly.

There are different attractive forces between molecules that hold them together in the liquid. You are familiar with the attraction of one pole of a magnet with the opposite pole of another, or the attraction of a magnet for a piece of iron. This is magnetic force. The force by which one water molecule attracts another is not a magnetic force but an electrical force, the attraction of a positive part of one molecule for a negative part of another. This force was called "holding hands" in the children's description. You may wish to elaborate with the more technical description which follows if you think it is appropriate for the children in your group.

Molecules like water, which have positive and negative parts, are called *polar*. They have a positive pole and a negative pole. See the following diagram. Molecules are composed of atoms. A water molecule is composed of two hydrogen atoms (H) and one oxygen atom (O). The *formula* for a water molecule is H_2O. The subscript 2 after the symbol H means that two hydrogens are present in the molecule. In water molecules the hydrogen atoms are positive poles and the oxygen atom is the negative pole.

Water molecules move throughout the liquid as attractive forces between them are relatively weak. Some molecules are moving slowly and some more rapidly. The motion and

Water molecules with positive and negative poles

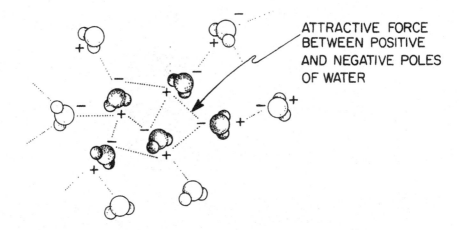

ATTRACTIVE FORCE
BETWEEN POSITIVE
AND NEGATIVE POLES
OF WATER

weakness of the attraction makes the liquid fluid. As a result, it changes shape easily, taking the shape of the container which holds it, unlike a solid which has its own shape.

Ways of representing a water molecule composed of one oxygen atom and two hydrogen atoms

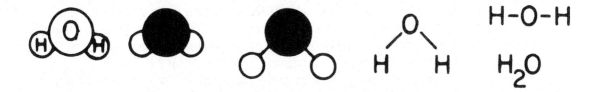

The surface of the liquid not touched by the container is flat because there are no attractive forces above the surface molecules to pull them up. There are only attractive forces from molecules underneath, as well as gravity, pulling them down. However, individual molecules in the surface layer which are moving very rapidly can leave the main body of the liquid and float into the air above the surface. At normal room temperature, only a few are moving fast enough to

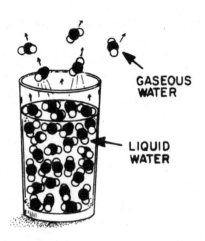

GASEOUS WATER

LIQUID WATER

leave. When they do enter the space above the surface they are invisible because they are so small and the spaces between them are so large.

The few molecules above the liquid, separated by large spaces and by air molecules (mainly nitrogen and oxygen), are the gaseous form of water, often called water vapor. If water in its liquid form is not covered, over a period of time all of the liquid water will change to gaseous water and disappear into the atmosphere. Water molecules which were close together and thus visible in the liquid become very far apart and invisible in the vapor. The change from liquid water to gaseous water, which takes place over a long time at normal everyday temperatures, is called evaporation. One of the dictionary definitions of evaporation is "to disappear." Now you can see how this disappearing act happens!

When water changes from its liquid to its gaseous form, this is called a *change of state*. Evaporation is one kind of change of state. We will talk about other changes of state in the chapters to follow.

Heat makes molecules move more rapidly. In fact, one way of defining heat is in terms of molecular motion (see Chapter 7). As the *temperature* of the liquid water increases, the *average speed* of all the water molecules increases. Water molecules at the surface can escape more easily. The rate of evaporation thus increases with increasing temperature. On a hot day a puddle will disappear much more rapidly than on a cold day.

Where Drops Come From

Condensing

> Water vapor gets together in a cloud. When it gets big enough to form a drop, it does.

Bobby: Mommy, my glass of lemonade is leaking!

Mother: What do you mean leaking? Our glasses don't leak. Unless they're cracked, and your glass isn't cracked.

B: It is too leaking! You poured my ice cold lemonade a few minutes ago, and now there are drops of it all over the outside of the glass. Look, I can even write my name in it.

M: Are you sure lemonade is leaking through the glass?

B: Where else would it come from? It must come from the inside to the outside of the glass. I want to know how it does that. Hot chocolate doesn't leak out of my cup and soup doesn't leak out of my bowl. Why does lemonade leak out of my glass?

M: Are you sure it's lemonade? Did you taste it?

B: No, but I will. [Licks moisture from outside surface of glass] That's very strange. It doesn't taste like lemonade.

M: What does it taste like?

B: It doesn't have a taste . . . so I guess it's water. How can water in the lemonade leak out, but lemon and sugar stay inside the glass? It doesn't make sense.

M: Are you sure that water on the outside of the glass comes from the lemonade inside?

B: I don't know! Doesn't it? Where else could it come from?

M: Perhaps it's a bad glass. Wipe off the outside of your glass and pour your lemonade in a cup. Then fill the glass with hot chocolate. We'll see what happens.

B: Oᴋ! [Pours lemonade into cup, wipes outside of glass and fills it with hot chocolate]

M: What do you see?

B: That's strange. No water is leaking out of the glass of hot chocolate, but now the cup of lemonade is leaking. Yes! There are drops of water forming on the outside of the cup of lemonade! It must be the lemonade. It must push water out of the cup and glass.

M: Wait a minute. This is confusing. I don't think it has anything to do with lemons or chocolate or sugar. What else could be causing it?

B: Well, maybe it's because the lemonade is cold and the chocolate is hot.

M: Oᴋ, let's take two new glasses and fill one with ice water and one with hot water. Then we'll look at the outside of each glass.

B: That's a good idea. [Takes two empty glasses and fills one with ice water and the other with hot water from the tap]

M: What do you see?

B: Well, this is very interesting. The glass of ice water is leaking through the glass; the glass of hot water isn't.

M: So it must have something to do with hot and cold, not chocolate or lemonade.

B: Yes, that's it.

M: But I still don't think the water is leaking through the glass.

B: But then where does it come from?

M: I've got an idea to help us find out. Let's fill your Mickey Mouse® glass right up to the top of Mickey Mouse's ears with ice water. Then we'll keep wiping off the water on the outside of the glass and see how much the level drops inside

37

the glass. It should go below Mickey Mouse's ears if water is leaking out.

B: That's a good idea. I'll do it out on the back patio on the picnic table. [Takes Mickey Mouse® glass, a pitcher of ice water, and a towel out to the picnic table]

M: Well, what happened? What did you see?

B: The water on the outside of the glass doesn't come from the inside.

M: How do you know?

B: I wiped water off the glass fifteen times. Every time I wiped it off it came right back. But the water inside the glass didn't drop below Mickey's ear. It didn't move at all. And the towel is really damp.

M: So water isn't leaking out of the glass?

B: That's right.

M: So it must be coming from somewhere else.

B: But where could it come from? It would have to come from the air. How could that be? Is there water in the air?

M: You should go ask Diana. She and your father had a long talk about that yesterday.

B: They did?

M: Yes. Diana wanted to know where puddles go, and she found out that little bits of water from the puddle go up into the air on a hot day. They're so small you can't see them. It's called evaporation. When puddles disappear they evaporate.

B: I'll go ask her.

M: Well, is there invisible water in the air?

B: Yes there is. And when the tiny bits of water are far apart in the air you can't see them. On a humid day, I think there are lots of water bits in the air. I feel very hot and sticky on humid days, and that's when the most water forms on cold glasses of lemonade.

M: So how come you can see them on the side of your glass of lemonade?

38

B: It's because of the cold glass. Diana said the water bits move around in the air very fast on a hot day and slow down on cold days. When they hit the cold glass I bet they slow down. In fact, some of them probably slow down enough to stick to the glass.

M: Then they would probably collect there.

B: Yes! And when a whole bunch of them collect together in a lump—all very close together—you can *see* them!

M: Yes, I think you're right. When water bits do this—when they come together to form a visible drop of water—it's called condensation. It's just the opposite of what puddles do when they disappear.

B: Is it like rain from clouds?

M: Something like that, yes!

B: How is it like clouds and rain?

M: Clouds are large collections of very tiny droplets of water. They form from the water bits when they slow down enough to collect together. They're so small and light that they float in the air.

B: Is a cloud water vapor?

M: No, because water vapor is invisible. You can see clouds.

B: Like I can see fog? Is a cloud like a fog?

M: Yes, like fog. And when those tiny droplets in the cloud collect together they form a bigger drop which is much heavier than the tiny droplet.

B: And then the bigger drop falls as rain? It's a raindrop?

M: Yes, it falls. It's a raindrop!!

Condensing–A Description

ir is composed of small bits so tiny and far apart from each other that we can't see them. But we know they are there when the wind blows and when we blow up a balloon. The blowing is the motion of large numbers of these bits, and we can feel and hear them when they move! We call things like air *gases*. As you learned in Chapter 1, when water bits are far apart they are also a gas, called water vapor. The bits in the vapor are also invisible because they are so small and far apart from each other. The bits in water vapor move rapidly, bumping into each other, into bits of air, and into the sides of any container they are in. They are moving so fast they never come together into a large pile so we can't see them. If you can think of them as having hands, they never could hold on to each other as they fly about. If the container they are in has no lid, they spread out and scatter into the atmosphere.

When water vapor comes into contact with a very cold surface, like the side of a glass of lemonade and ice, the cold slows the bits so much that they collect together on the surface of the glass and form a visible film of liquid water. It is as if they began holding hands with each other. Eventually the film can slide down the side of the glass and form a drop. Water vapor which does this is said to be *condensing*; it is water changing from its vapor form (with bits far apart) to its liquid form (with bits close together). The bits in the vapor have come together or *condensed* into the liquid.

Condensation is the *opposite of* the process called *evaporation*, the topic of Chapter 1. Cooling water vapor makes it condense. It slows down the moving bits of water so they can collect together in a pile and become visible liquid water. Heating liquid water makes it evaporate faster, because it speeds up the moving water bits in the liquid so they can escape into the air as water vapor. See the description of evaporation in Chapter 1 for a review.

When it's cold enough, water vapor can condense onto tiny pieces of dust floating in the sky forming a tiny droplet around each dust particle. A large collection of these tiny droplets is visible as a cloud. When a lot of these droplets come together they form a much bigger visible drop, which is much heavier than the very tiny droplet. This drop can fall from the sky as rain.

Condensing

| glass of ice cold lemonade—just poured | glass of ice cold lemonade—after 30 seconds | glass of ice cold lemonade—after 1 minute | glass of ice cold lemonade—after 2 minutes |

Experiments

YOU WILL NEED:
glasses
pot
Styrofoam® cups
pot lids
cold water
hot water
cooking oil
hot chocolate

 Carefully dry the outside of a glass of ice cold water. Hold it above a pot of very hot water and look at the bottom of the glass. **(Have a parent help you, and be careful not to burn yourself!)** What do you see? Repeat the experiment with a glass of hot water. Is the result different? What do you think is happening? Why might the glass of cold water be different than the glass of hot water?

CAUTION: Have a parent help you with this experiment

ICE WATER

POT OF
VERY HOT
WATER →

 Try the same experiment with a Styrofoam® cup of cold water instead of a glass. Are the results the same? Why might the Styrofoam® cup experiment be different? What do you notice about how your hand feels when it holds hot and cold liquids in a Styrofoam® cup compared to hot and cold liquids in a glass? What does Styrofoam® do?

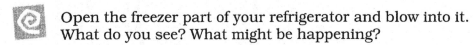 Open the freezer part of your refrigerator and blow into it. What do you see? What might be happening?

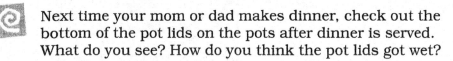 Next time your mom or dad makes dinner, check out the bottom of the pot lids on the pots after dinner is served. What do you see? How do you think the pot lids got wet?

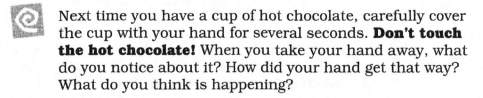 Next time you have a cup of hot chocolate, carefully cover the cup with your hand for several seconds. **Don't touch the hot chocolate!** When you take your hand away, what do you notice about it? How did your hand get that way? What do you think is happening?

Do the same experiment with a glass of hot water. Are the results the same as with the hot chocolate? Do you think the same thing would happen with a cup of hot soup? Why or why not? Try and think of an explanation for what you observe.

 Next time you take a shower, rub a small bit of cooking oil on the bathroom mirror before you get in the shower. **(Get permission from your mom or dad first!)** After your shower is over, see if the mirror fogs up. Is the part of the mirror with the oil on it different from the other part of the mirror? If it is, what might be happening?

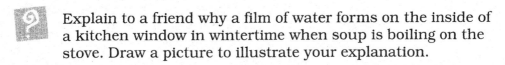

Questions to Write and Draw

Explain to a friend why a film of water forms on the inside of a kitchen window in wintertime when soup is boiling on the stove. Draw a picture to illustrate your explanation.

How are clouds and rain like the water which forms on the outside of a glass of cold soda?

Why does your breath look like a white cloud when you breathe out on a very cold day? What must your breath contain for it to form a white cloud?

Why do car windows "fog up" on very cold nights when a lot of people get in the car?

Why does the bottom of the lid on a bowl of steaming spaghetti get water drops all over it? Where do the drops come from?

How does morning dew form on grass and flowers?

Why does mist form above rivers on cold mornings?

Use diagrams to help illustrate your explanations to some of the above questions. Remember the different forms of water, and how the water bits behave in each form.

For Parents and Teachers

Getting Started

A good way of getting started on a discussion of condensation is to hold a pan of ice cubes over a container of hot or steaming water. Vapor will condense on the bottom of the pan. Have children examine the bottom of the pan before and after you hold it over the hot water. Collect their descriptions of the pan both before and after on a blackboard or a piece of paper. Then ask for suggestions about what is happening: "Where is the water on the bottom of the pan coming from?" Generate another list of their explanations which you can examine together.

Children often think the melting ice cubes are leaking through small holes in the pan. You can have them test that hypothesis by carefully drying the pan completely, filling it with warm water, and examining it for leaks. There will be none, unless you happen to be using a pan which does have holes in it! Focus their discussion on explanations which involve hot water traveling, in some way, to the bottom of the pan: "Could the hot water get to the bottom of the cold pan?"

You can generate more discussion with this question which will lead towards the dialogue between Bobby and his mom. You or the children could read and discuss it. The relationship to ideas covered in Chapter 1, on evaporation, are drawn out in the dialogue. Talk about these again with the children. Bring in other examples of condensation at this point, like fogged mirrors in the bathroom after a hot shower or clouding car windows on a cold night when lots of people are in the car.

A Deeper Look

Molecules in a gas are very far apart from each other. A description of water in its gaseous state was elaborated on in Chapter 1. A substance in its gaseous state spreads out to

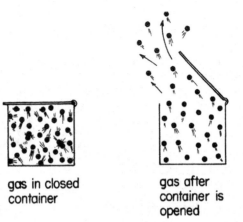

gas in closed
container

gas after
container is
opened

fill any closed container. If it is in the open atmosphere, it becomes dispersed.

Molecules in a gas move very rapidly, bouncing off each other and off the container walls. These rapidly moving molecules have high kinetic energy. Kinetic energy is energy of motion. The higher the temperature the faster molecules move and the higher their kinetic energy.

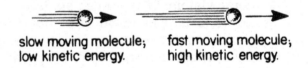

slow moving molecule;
low kinetic energy.

fast moving molecule;
high kinetic energy.

Air is a gas. We become more aware of it when we blow up a balloon. Air molecules bouncing against the inside of the balloon keep it inflated. Hot air will make a balloon bigger than an equal amount of cold air because air molecules move more rapidly in hot air, hitting the inside of the balloon harder and pushing it farther out. You can easily demonstrate this by measuring the diameter of a balloon with a string, and quickly measuring it again after it's been in the freezer for an hour.

As the temperature is lowered, gas molecules slow down. They have less kinetic energy. If the temperature is low

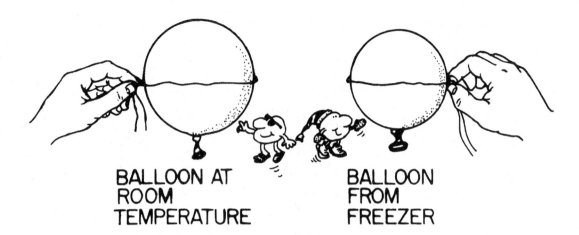

BALLOON AT
ROOM
TEMPERATURE

BALLOON
FROM
FREEZER

enough, and there is a cold surface where the molecules can collect, they will stick to the surface and collect together. The attractive forces between molecules can then begin to hold them together. The kinetic energy of molecules in the liquid (their motion in the liquid) is much less than the kinetic energy of molecules in the gas (motion of molecules in the gas).

If enough water molecules collect on a surface they become visible. When a gas such as water vapor changes to its liquid form, this is called a *change of state* from the gas to the liquid phase. This concept was first introduced in Chapter 1 where the process of evaporation was a change of state of water from its liquid to its gaseous form. The change of state of gaseous substances to their liquid form is called *condensation*. It is the reverse of the process of evaporation. Invisible molecules that are far apart come together in a very large collection that can be seen. For children, the most commonly experienced type of condensation is that of invisible water vapor condensing to visible liquid water.

Steam is actually a collection of very small water droplets, and these are visible as a white vapor (see the discussion of clouds below). Steam is not really gaseous water. In true gaseous water, molecules are not collected together in a drop of any size. They are individual molecules with large spaces between them and are invisible. When liquid water is heated you will often see steam first. This quickly changes to gaseous water as steam is dispersed into the air and the tiny droplets come apart into individual molecules. The intermediate state of steam does not form during the process of slow evaporation, but is more commonly seen during boiling when water is heated to much higher temperatures (see Chapter 8).

At very, very low temperatures, almost two hundred degrees below zero centigrade, gaseous air can be condensed to liquid air. Normal temperatures on the surface of the earth do not go this low, however, so we only experience air in its liquid state under laboratory conditions where very low temperatures can be generated safely. Children who view a large container of liquid air call it "very cold water." It is very difficult for them to conceive of air condensing to the liquid state. Their experience of liquid water is all encompassing and they have no experience of the behavior of substances at temperatures of two hundred degrees below zero centigrade. On the other hand, gaseous water vapor easily changes to liquid at temperatures commonly experienced in everyday life.

Air is composed mainly of oxygen gas and nitrogen gas, with smaller, variable amounts of carbon dioxide gas, water gas (vapor), and other gases. The amount of water vapor in air is measured by the *humidity*. The higher the humidity, the more water vapor is in the air.

When the air contains gaseous water, water molecules colliding with the cold surface of a glass of iced drink will slow down sufficiently to stick to it. When enough water molecules do this, they will collect as a visible film of liquid water which can slide down the side of the glass and form drops. This is most apparent on humid days. Some children, seeing this, believe that the liquid is coming from the inside of the glass because water vapor in the air is invisible. It seems to make more sense that visible water on the inside of the glass somehow gets to be visible water on the outside. Thus the glass must have a leak! Most children have indeed experienced or created a leaking paper cup. The experiments noted earlier in this chapter are designed to help children overcome the misconception that water can come through an intact glass.

The process that occurs on the side of a glass also occurs in the sky. In this case, the surface is not a glass, but small dust particles. The resulting clouds are composed of large numbers of very tiny water droplets, so small that they float. When these very tiny droplets collect together they form a much bigger drop which falls as rain.

Seeding clouds with silver iodide dust is a way of speeding the formation of larger drops. Silver iodide provides a surface upon which the tiny droplets can collect to form a larger drop. Of course, silver iodide is not always necessary, since rain drops will form on their own. Where they do not, however, and where rain is desired, "seeding" clouds with silver iodide often helps. For example, if farmers need more rain for their crops during a drought, clouds might be seeded to help rain form.

Disappearing in the Drink

Dissolving

" *To most people solutions mean finding the answers. But to chemists solutions are things that are still all mixed up.* "

Jose: Hey, Ma, look at this!!

Mother: Look at what, water? Hey, Jose . . . what are you doing with all that sugar? It's not good to eat plain sugar, especially so much all at one time! Now put it back in the box please. And don't make a mess.

 **J:** No, please, Ma! Look at this. Bobby and I found this out at his house when we were making lemonade for our lemonade stand. Tell me why this happens.

M: Why what happens? Does Bobby's mother know about this lemonade stand?

J: Yes, Ma. Now look. Please look at this. Here's a half a glass of water and a half a glass of sugar. Now watch this.

M: What are you doing? Hey . . . that much sugar is going to make it too sweet! You won't like it. Your customers won't buy it.

J: Gee whiz, Ma, this isn't for lemonade. Look! I mix a half a glass of water with half a glass of sugar and stir it up and. . . .

M: Sugar water. Very sweet I might add. Too sweet.

J: Yes, Ma. You already said that. But look at it. It's odd.

52

M: What's odd about it. Doesn't look odd to me. It might taste odd though.

J: The sugar turns into water. Sand doesn't do that. But even more interesting—it doesn't add up!

M: What do you mean it doesn't add up?

J: The sugar and water. Half a glass and half a glass should make a whole glass. The sugar water doesn't come any-where near the top of the glass. . . . It's way down from the top.

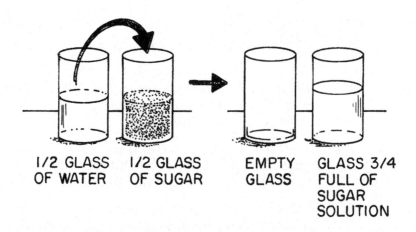

1/2 GLASS OF WATER 1/2 GLASS OF SUGAR EMPTY GLASS GLASS 3/4 FULL OF SUGAR SOLUTION

I mixed a half a glass of water with a half a glass of sugar and something is missing! So tell me where it went. And why does the sugar change to water when I put it in water? And why don't I get a whole glass of sugar water?

M: Hold on a minute, Jose. You're asking too many questions. Slow down.

J: Ok! Tell me why it all turns to water. Sand doesn't do that. It just sinks to the bottom of the glass.

M: Is the sugar water the same as regular water?

J: Well, not really. It's sweet, of course. And thicker . . . kind of syrupy.

M: Then the sugar really didn't turn into water did it?

J: Not regular water. Kind of a thicker water. And sweeter.

M: Ok, so let's look really closely at what's going on. Let's use this rock candy. It's pure sugar you know. Just in bigger chunks.

J: I like that stuff. It tastes great and it's pretty, like crystals.

M: Ok. So put a piece in a glass of water and look at it carefully!

J: [Drops a piece in a glass of water]

The water is full of swirls and twists near the crystal. It looks like something is coming off, like a clear smoke. It's hard to see clearly now right next to the crystal. It's very wavy looking.

M: So mix it up a bit.

J: [Mixes water and rock candy with a spoon]

The swirls are all through the water, and now—now they are disappearing. It looks neat. Wait, they're starting again right near the crystal. But the rock candy—the crystal—is changed. It looks smaller!

M: Swirl it one more time and pour the liquid out into another glass. But don't pour out the crystal. When it starts to come out, hold it back with your finger.

J: Ok! [Pours the liquid into another glass through his fingers, grabbing the remains of the rock candy as it slides down the side of the upturned glass]

M: Now what does the rock candy look like?

J: It's wet.

M: Of course it's wet. It just came out of a glass of water. What does it look like? Is it different from the crystal that you put in originally?

J: You mean in addition to being wet?

M: Yes!

J: Well . . . it looks a bit lumpy now. It isn't as nice as when I put it in.

M: Anything else?

J: Hmm. I don't know. Wait. Yes, it's smaller. Definitely—it is smaller.

M: Well, what would that mean?

J: I don't know. Does it mean that some of it changed to water? Sweet water? Like ice melts? Is that what's happening? When I put ice in water, eventually it all changes to water. Yes, that must be it. The sugar melts.

M: But ice melts all by itself when you take it out of the freezer. Sugar doesn't do that. It just sits there until you put it in water.

J: So—it's not the same as ice melting?

M: No, it isn't.

J: But the sugar is changing.

M: Yes it is. But the change is not the same as melting.

J: So what is happening? What is the sugar crystal doing? Maybe the water is melting it.

M: What causes melting, Jose?

J: Warming. When ice gets warm it melts.

M: But you didn't warm the sugar, you just put it in water.

J: Ok, I give up. What's happening? The same thing happens with salt. I tried that yesterday. And just like the water got sweet with sugar, it got salty with salt. And it looked like the salt melted, just like the sugar melted.

M: It's not melting, remember.

J: It looks like melting.

M: It's called dissolving.

J: Dissolving?

M: Yes.

J: That's no help at all! *I want to know what's happening!*

M: Go look up the word "dissolve" in the dictionary.

J: In the dictionary?! Oh Ma, come on. [pause] I'm going over to Bobby's to fix up our lemonade stand.

M: Come on Jose, do it for me. Then you'll understand.

J: Ok, but then you'll explain it to me?

M: I will.

J: Ok. [Goes to dictionary]

M: What does it say?

J: It says all kinds of stuff.

M: So pick out some of the words.

J: "Coming apart or breaking up." That's a simple one.

M: Why, that's perfect.

J: Why is that?

M: Because that is just what the sugar is doing in water; it's breaking up.

J: It is? It doesn't look like it's breaking up. It looks like it's melting.

M: You're right! It does *look like* it's melting, and that's what fools everyone. Because when it breaks apart the pieces are so small you can't see them!

J: Even with a magnifying glass?

M: Yes, Jose. The sugar is formed from a very large number of tiny bits all stacked together in a shape called a crystal. When you put the crystal in water the little bits come apart from each other and sort of swim away. When the bits are far apart you can't see the sugar crystals anymore. They disappear because the bits are so small they're invisible

It's not the same as melting. The sugar water is called a solution of sugar in water.

J: How come sand doesn't dissolve like sugar? Why don't tiny sand bits swim away from the sand crystal?

M: Because the attraction between the tiny sand bits in a sand crystal is much stronger than the attraction between tiny sugar bits in a sugar crystal. So the sugar comes apart easier.

J: Ok. And why doesn't half a glass of water and half a glass of sugar give a whole glass of sugar water?

M: Partly because there is space between the small bits in the sugar crystals. There must also be some space in the water. These extra spaces must fill up when the sugar water is formed. I'm not really sure about that though.

J: You mean you don't know?! I don't see any spaces in water.

M: Yes, Jose, I know. I don't either. I'm not really sure. Let's talk about it some more tomorrow.

J: OK, Ma. We're selling lemonade tomorrow. Will you buy some?

M: I already bought some.

J: No you didn't!

M: Yes, I bought it at the grocery store. You're using the lemons, sugar, and paper cups that I bought last week, and . . .

J: Oh, Ma, come on!

M: OK, Jose, I'll buy a glass. Maybe you'll make enough profit to buy some lemons and sugar.

J: Gee whiz, then I won't make any money!

M: So I'm subsidizing you, is that it?

J: Subsidizing. What's that?

M: Later, Jose, later, OK?

Dissolving–A Description

Dissolving occurs when the closely stacked bits of a solid, like sugar, break away from each other and mix into a liquid, like water. If you can think of the sugar bits as holding on tight to each other in the solid sugar, when they dissolve in water they let go of each other and begin to hold hands with the water. We call the mixture a *solution* of sugar in water. The sugar bits are now

57

holding hands with water and not with each other. When completely formed, the solution is the same throughout (if we use enough water, no visible sugar is left). The solid seems to have disappeared into the liquid. It looks like the sugar melted into the water, but it is not melting. Melting requires heat. Dissolving can be speeded up by heat, and hot liquids often dissolve more solid than cold liquids, but heat is not always necessary for dissolving to occur. When liquid water dissolves things it's called a *solvent*. Things which dissolve in water, like sugar or salt, are called the *solute*. When something doesn't dissolve very well in water it is called *insoluble*. Sand is insoluble in water. When something does dissolve in water it is called *soluble*. Sugar is soluble in water.

As we noted above, a solid material such as sugar is also a large collection of bits, just like a liquid. However, in a solid the bits do not move about from place to place like in the liquid, but are rigidly held in place—much like eggs in a carton—to form a *crystal*. (We will learn more about this in Chapter 7.) In a solid, you can think of the bits as hugging each other very tightly, much more tightly than the bits in a liquid like water. This is why the solid holds its own crystalline shape, whereas a liquid such as water, where the bits move around more, takes the shape of its container.

When solid sugar, the solute, is added to liquid water, the solvent, rapidly moving water bits collide with the sides of the sugar crystal knocking off tiny bits of sugar. These sugar bits then move and wander throughout the water and become separated from each other. Water bits keep on hitting the sides of the sugar crystal, dislodging more and more sugar bits. The sugar crystal gets smaller and smaller as sugar bits keep coming off until eventually all of the crystal is broken down. The sugar bits wander separately throughout the liquid water, and a *solution* of sugar in water results. The sugar bits are no longer close together as they were in the sugar crystal. Instead, they are far apart. The spaces between them are filled with water bits. The sugar is said to have *dissolved* in the water. Though we can't see it anymore, we can taste it, because a solution of sugar in water is sweet.

Sometimes when a solid dissolves in a liquid, the solution takes up less space than the original solid and liquid do. This happens when sugar dissolves in water. So if you mix a half a glass of water and a half a glass of sugar, the solution doesn't fill the glass. This is because there are spaces between the tiny sugar crystals in the half a glass of sugar. Also, the sugar and water bits hold on very tightly to each other in the solution, much tighter than to themselves in pure sugar or pure water. So the solution takes up less space.

Dissolving

| sugar crystal before the water is added | sugar crystal dissolving in water 1 minute after the water is added | sugar crystal dissolving in water 3 minutes after the water is added | a solution of sugar in water |

Experiments

Fill two small glasses half full of water. Make sure you fill each one to the same level. In one glass, add teaspoons of salt, one at a time while stirring, until no more will dissolve. Keep a record of the number of teaspoons you add. In the other glass of water, do the same thing with teaspoons of sugar.

COUNT TEASPOONS
OF SALT ADDED WITH
STIRRING UNTIL NO
MORE WILL DISSOLVE.

COUNT TEASPOONS
OF SUGAR ADDED WITH
STIRRING UNTIL NO
MORE WILL DISSOLVE.

 How many teaspoons of salt dissolve? How many teaspoons of sugar? Which is more soluble in water, salt or sugar?

 Dissolve as much salt as you can in a small glass of very hot water from the faucet. Be careful not to burn yourself. **(Have a parent help you!)** Cover the glass of hot salt solution and put it in the icebox. Leave it there until you see something forming in the glass. This might happen overnight or it might take a week, so be patient. Carefully observe the results. What happens? Why do you think it happens? Is salt more soluble in hot water or cold water?

 Drop a large crystal of rock candy in a glass of water and see how long it takes to completely dissolve when you stir it with a spoon. Do it again with another glass containing the same amount of water, using a crystal the same size as the first one. But before you add it to the water, grind it up into very small pieces. You can do this between two spoons.

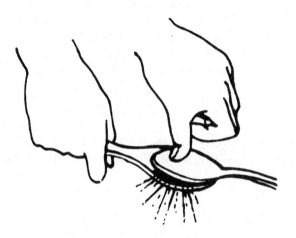

 Does the ground up crystal dissolve faster or slower than the one you didn't grind up? Why or why not? Are there more places on the sugar crystal for water to touch it when it is large or when it is all broken up into small pieces? (Hint: For water to dissolve a crystal it must come in contact with the crystal surface. Is there more crystal surface on a large crystal or on the many pieces you get when you grind it up?)

 Make up a mixture of equal parts of sand and salt. Design and carry out an experiment which will allow you to get them into separate piles, one of salt and one of sand.

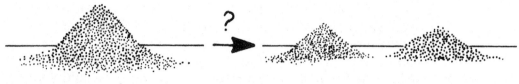

**mixture of
salt and sand**   **salt**   **sand**

 Make a list of other solvents, besides water, that might be useful for dissolving things? **With your parents' permission** put a small amount of nail polish remover in a small glass. Make sure you do this in a room where the windows are open, or do it outside. Take a polystyrene cup and break it up into pieces. Put a few of the smaller pieces in the nail polish remover. Describe what happens. (Flush the mixture down the toilet when you are done or pour it into a carton or container with a lid and put it in the trash.) What is the solvent in this experiment? What is the solute?

 Will salt dissolve in vegetable oil? Will baking soda? Will baking soda dissolve in water? Try these experiments and see.

Questions to Write and Draw

 Why might hot water dissolve sugar *faster* than cold water? Why might hot water dissolve *more* sugar than cold water? Draw a diagram showing the movement of the small bits of water which illustrates your explanations. Go back to Chapter 1 and look at how water bits move when water is cold and when it is hot. Can you design a simple experiment, using hot and cold water from the faucet, to prove that hot water dissolves more sugar than cold water?

 How fast sugar dissolves depends on the amount of the sugar crystal's *surface* exposed to water. A large crystal of sugar in water dissolves much more slowly than an equal amount of sugar in the form of many small crystals. Go back and review the experiment you did dissolving the large crystal of rock candy. Which has more surface area, one large sugar crystal or an equal amount of sugar broken into small pieces? Can you illustrate this by drawing a picture?

 Make a list of things you know dissolve in water (soluble things) and another list of things you know do not dissolve in water (insoluble things). Is there anything all the soluble things have in common? How about the insoluble things? Do they have anything in common?

 What do you think would happen if you dissolved two tablespoons of salt in a small amount of water and poured it out on a plate and let it sit for a week? Make a diagram showing tiny bits of salt and water, illustrating what happens over time. You could do this by drawing several pictures, each representing the plate of salt water at a different time.

Next time you go to the grocery store, make a list of the liquids you see which might be solutions. Make a list of the liquids you see which have insoluble solids floating in them or solids sitting on the bottom of the container. Liquids which have insoluble solids floating in them are called *suspensions* of a solid in a liquid. The solids float, or are *suspended,* in the liquid.

 What two different liquids from the kitchen will dissolve in each other? What two different liquids from the kitchen will not dissolve in each other? What happens when you stir together two liquids that don't dissolve in each other? Do not mix any cleaning solutions together!

 What drinks are made by dissolving solids in water?

For Parent and Teachers

Getting Started

Children will be very interested in learning about dissolving and solutions if you have them make lemon flavored Kool-Aid®. It is best to use lemon flavor so that the color will not keep them from seeing the powder dissolve. Use pre-sweetened Kool-Aid® and the crystal clear plastic glasses sold in supermarkets so they can see what happens and can drink the end product of their experiments.

Give each child two clear plastic glasses, one containing the amount of Kool-Aid® powder needed to make one cup of flavored drink when water is added, and one full of water. Ask them to carefully pour the water into the glass with the powder. Without stirring the mixture, have them record their observations in both words and pictures. Collect their observations on the blackboard, overhead, or piece of paper. Get as many comments as you can. These will express the visual process of dissolving in their own words. The dissolving process will take a while and changes observed over time should be part of your discussion. For example, does the mixture look the same right after the water is added as it does in twenty minutes?

If, after twenty or thirty minutes, there is still solid at the bottom of the glass, have them stir the mixture until the powder is completely gone. Pose the question: "Where did the Kool-Aid® powder go?" Collect responses and list them again. Focus and elaborate on those closest to the descriptive comments on dissolving. This leads into the dialogue between Jose and his mom.

A Deeper Look

Different kinds of solids have different properties, but the process by which they dissolve in a liquid are similar. The ordered array of the crystal breaks down and the individual bits become separated from each other, mixing in with the bits of liquid.

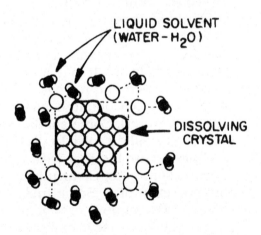

The crystal disappears and a solution of the solid in the liquid is formed. The solid which dissolves is called the *solute*. The liquid which dissolves the solute is called the *solvent*. Where it is not obvious which is the solute and which is the solvent (for example, if two liquids are dissolved in each other), it is the convention to name the larger component of the solution the solvent and the lesser component the solute.

Visual observations of a large solid crystal dissolving in a liquid solvent clearly show it diminishing in size as it goes into solution. This is hard to see for a collection of very small crystals like ordinary table salt or table sugar. In either case, however, the rigid array breaks down at the crystal surface as rapidly moving solvent molecules crash into it. In this collision the solvent molecules knock particles out of the fixed array at the crystal surface. These then become surrounded by solvent molecules and move throughout the solution. Visually it looks like melting, but it isn't (see Chapter 7 for details of the melting process).

Crystals of salt or sugar completely dissolved in water are *homogeneous mixtures.* There is no evidence of any remaining solid (if sufficient water is added). The properties of the solution are different from those of the liquid and solid from which it is formed. The saltwater solution contains ions and conducts electricity. The sugar water solution contains neutral molecules and does not. Mixtures are discussed in detail in Chapter 5.

Liquid solutes can also dissolve in liquid solvents to give solutions (i.e., alcohol in water), and gaseous solutes can dissolve in gaseous solvents to give solutions. Air is an example of the latter. It is a solution containing mainly gaseous oxygen and nitrogen. Gases can dissolve in liquid solvents also (carbonated water is a solution of carbon dioxide gas in water). Some solids will even dissolve gases (hydrogen gas will dissolve in platinum metal).

Children are familiar with many different types of homogeneous solutions. Clear juices and drinks are the most common examples. Sometimes liquids contain suspended solids. An example is orange juice. Orange juice is called a *suspension* because it has solid floating in it. If the solid sinks to the bottom, it isn't really a suspension. It's just a liquid with an insoluble or partially soluble substance in it. Clear juices are examples of solutions which contain sugar, flavors, pigments, and other nutrients completely dissolved in water.

Appearing in the Drink

Crystallizing

" Crystals grow and grow, but you never have to feed them. "

Maria: Daddy, Daddy, Jose's old lemonade made ants! He left it on the patio table last weekend, and now there are ants in the glass. Yuck!

Father: What do you mean, made ants?

M: The lemonade is gone and there's gooey white stuff in the bottom of the glass with ants all over it. It looks yucky!

F: You think lemonade made ants?

M: No, I guess not. The ants are walking around in the glass though.

F: Where do you think they came from?

M: They're on the table and on the patio too. And there's a line of ants all the way to the garden. What's the white stuff in the glass, Daddy?

F: Must be something ants like to walk around in. What do you think it might be? Why would ants come to walk around in it?

M: It's from the lemonade. Should I squish the ants?

F: Just shake them out of the glass on the lawn. If the white stuff is from lemonade, what is it?

M: Sugar and lemon stuff? Maybe that's why the ants like it.

F: So where's the water?

M: It disappeared. Probably like a puddle disappears. Diana told me how that happens. It's called evaporation. When water bits escape into the air they turn into vapor which is invisible.

F: Why didn't the sugar and lemon stuff evaporate and disappear?

M: But sugar is solid and solid things don't evaporate, do they?

F: Not usually.

M: So the white stuff in the glass is mainly sugar, mixed with stuff from lemons?

F: Must be so!

M: That's why the ants like it, Daddy. It must taste good. Though I can't really see them eating it, even when I look real close.

F: It is kind of hard to see an ant's mouth isn't it?

M: I'll taste it myself to see if [reaches in glass to scrape out white residue]. . . .

F: Maria! *Stop!* It's been sitting outside here on the patio for a week. And it's got ants all over it, and you're going to eat it?

M: Well—maybe I shouldn't.

F: No, you shouldn't. It's dirty now. It's been there a week.

M: So how will I know if it's sugar and lemon stuff?

F: If you're patient, we can try an experiment. We'll do it inside the house so ants won't get in it. And we'll put it in a place where dust won't drop in it either.

M: Can we do it in my room, Daddy, please?

F: We'll make it in the kitchen and then carry it to your room, OK?

M: Yes! Let's do it now.

[Both go inside to the kitchen. They get a glass dinner plate out of the cabinet]

F: Let's do it with salt instead of sugar.

M: But why? It won't taste as good.

F: Because sometimes sugar doesn't work as well. It forms a syrup which takes a long time to crystallize, like the gooey stuff in Jose's glass. I'll explain later. Let's do it with salt first. You can try sugar after we do salt. Run the hot water faucet till the water is really hot.

[Maria turns on the hot water faucet, letting the water run]

M: Ok. It's hot.

F: Now take this small glass and fill it half full with hot water. Then pour in salt right out of the cardboard salt container into the glass of hot water until the water is almost to the top of the glass.

M: Ok. I did it. We are dissolving the salt, aren't we Daddy?

F: Yes, we are.

M: Jose told me about dissolving. But we put too much salt in. Some is sitting in the bottom of the glass of water.

F: I know that. I want to get as much salt in the hot water as we can. Now stir it up with a spoon for a minute or so, and let the solid salt that doesn't dissolve settle to the bottom.

M: Ok, I'm done.

F: Now—carefully pour the clear liquid off the top into the dinner plate. But don't pour any of the solid salt out of the glass.

M: I did it. But it looks a bit cloudy.

F: That's just a tiny bit of powder the salt makers mix in with the salt to keep it from clumping together on humid days. We'll ignore it, ok? It doesn't dissolve. Even in hot water.

M: So now what do we do?

F: We carry the plate of hot salt water to your room. I'll do it for you.

[They walk to Maria's room very slowly so the solution doesn't spill]

M: Put it on my desk, Daddy.

F: But then you won't be able to do your homework.

M: That's OK, I'll do it in the living room.

F: In front of the TV?

M: Yes, that's a good idea!

F: I'd prefer you do it in your room. Let's put the solution here on your bookcase.

M: Put it on the top shelf.

F: There!

M: Now what?

F: We wait.

M: Wait? How long do we wait?

F: It's hard to say. Maybe a few hours. Maybe a day or two.

M: I'll sit here and watch. What's going to happen?

F: It takes a long time Maria. You don't want to sit and watch it. You can check it each day. And remember, be patient. It might be quite a while before you see anything interesting.

M: Tell me what's going to happen. What will I see?

F: It's called crystallization. I think we should just let it happen and you can tell me what you see when it does. Now, let's go have lunch.

[They leave Maria's room and go back into the kitchen and make sandwiches.]

[The next evening]

M: Daddy, Daddy—it's happening.

F: What?

M: Crystallization! Come and look. There are little white pieces all around the edge of the water.

F: It's called a solution, Maria. There are little white pieces all around the edge of the solution. And what are the white pieces?

M: They must be salt, because the water is evaporating and the salt isn't. Can I take one and taste it?

F: If you wish, sure.

M: Yes. It's salt all right. [Makes a face]

F: Now leave the plate alone and we'll look at it again in the morning when you get up.

M: It's bedtime already?

F: It is.

[The next morning]

M: Daddy! Wake up. There are little squares all over the plate in the solution. They came in the night.

F: Squares? What do you mean squares?

M: In the solution. There are little squares of all different sizes in the solution on the plate. And some of the squares have little cross lines on them. They don't look like salt from the salt shaker at all. They're much too big to fit through holes.

F: They're crystals of salt, Maria. They grew all night long.

M: They grew? How did they do that?

F: When we dissolved the salt, it came apart into tiny invisible bits which floated around in the water.

M: Then what happens?

F: When we let it sit for a long time the water slowly evaporates, but salt doesn't. This makes the tiny salt bits come closer together in the solution. When water evaporates there is less of it remaining behind in the solution. The salt bits don't evaporate, so there are more of them left in the solution compared to the water. When this happens we say the solution is getting more concentrated.

M: What about the little salt squares? Where do they come from?

F: After a while, there are so many salt bits and so few water bits in the solution that salt bits get together and form a crystal. The little squares are growing salt crystals. They form when the water leaves. They will form if a very hot concentrated solution of salt in water cools, even without evaporation. Though it can take longer.

M: How come the crystals don't look like salt in the box? The ones in the box are tiny grains.

F: Look at them carefully under your magnifying glass, Maria, and you will see that they do have a square shape. Actually they are cubes, very similar to the salt on the plate.

M: But why does salt in the box come in such tiny cubes?

F: The salt company breaks up big cubes and screens the salt to a uniform size. People like salt that way. It's easier to shake out of a salt shaker, isn't it? And it dissolves faster when you put it on your food. You wouldn't want to put a big cube of salt on your potato, would you? It wouldn't flavor it properly. It would just sit there.

M: I see.

F: Now, do you know how the white stuff in Jose's old glass of lemonade formed?

M: Yes, I think so. But I want to try it with sugar. I want to make some sugar crystals just like we made salt crystals. They taste better.

F: It's not as easy. The sugar bits are bigger than salt bits and water sticks to them very tightly. It has a harder time evaporating from a solution of sugar than from a solution of salt. Sometimes it turns into a syrup.

M: Like on pancakes? That's OK. I like syrup a lot. Can I try it? Please. Let me try it?

F: Ok. You try it all by yourself. Do the same thing we did with the salt and water, but substitute sugar instead. Leave out the lemon juice though. You'll also see that a lot more sugar dissolves in hot water than salt does. That's another reason it's harder to form crystals of sugar.

M: It doesn't matter, Daddy. Because if it doesn't work, you know what?

F: What?

M: I can put the syrup on my pancakes.

F: Ok, but keep the dust out of your dish. Put it on the inside shelf of your bookcase, not on the top. And tell your mother what you are doing, please. If you need help carrying the dish to your room, call me.

M: I will. I will.

Crystallizing–A Description

Remember what you learned about dissolving in Chapter 3? Dissolving occurs when a solid, like a sugar crystal, comes apart in a liquid like water. When the sugar bits are far apart in the solution you can't see them. Crystallization is just the opposite of dissolving. It occurs when the bits of solid in the solution come back together and stack themselves into a crystal. The dissolved solid seems to appear out of nowhere! It comes from dissolved bits of solid in the solution when it cools, or when we allow some of the water to evaporate.

In a sugar solution, the small bits of sugar never get together in a large enough collection to be seen. They are separated from each other by the water in the solution. Cooling the solution makes both sugar and water bits move more slowly, so the sugar bits have a better chance of sticking to each other. If you can think of them as having hands to hold, the cooler the solution, the easier it is for them to get together and hold hands. If we take more water out of the solution through evaporation, sugar bits have an even better chance of getting together since there is less water to keep them apart. If they can't hold hands with water, they have a greater chance of holding hands with each other. So when the water goes, the sugar bits are attracted to each other more than to the water. And there are so many that eventually enough of them get together to form a very tiny crystal which is visible. This crystal keeps collecting more and more bits of sugar on its surface. It's a growing crystal of sugar. In the sugar crystal the bits of sugar no longer move around. They are all stacked in unmoving rows next to one another, very much like Legos® in a Lego® house.

Salt, like sugar, can form crystals from a saltwater solution as the water evaporates off. They can also form if you dissolve as much salt as you can in very hot water and then cool the solution in the refrigerator.

Different kinds of crystals result from different substances. Salt crystals and sugar crystals, which form from salt water and sugar water solutions when the water evaporates, have different shapes. The shape of a crystal depends on the size and kind of bits which make it up. Some crystals are like little cubes. Others are like hexagons. Some are long and needle-like, whereas others are like octahedrons (a tile-like crystal with eight sides).

A hexagonal crystal

 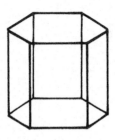

Crystals can also form when a pure liquid turns into a solid. When water freezes it forms a crystalline solid called ice. Snowflakes are beautiful crystals of frozen water. You'll learn more about how freezing liquids form crystals in Chapter 7.

Crystallizing

| a solution of salt in water | a solution of salt in water after 1 day | a solution of salt in water after 3 days | salt crystallizing out after 5 days |

Experiments

YOU WILL NEED:	large pot
a glass or clean plastic cup	salt
	hot water
clear glass plate or shallow clear glass bowl	sugar
	baking soda
	colorless diet soda
aluminum foil	
glass soup or cereal bowl	colorless regular soda
nail	sea water
piece of string	

 Dissolve *as much salt as you can* in a glass of very hot water. Be very careful. **(Ask a parent for help if you need it!)** Pour some of the solution on a clear glass plate or a shallow clear glass bowl. If you don't have one in your house, you can get them at most kitchen supply stores. Pour the rest into a glass and cover it with aluminum foil. Put the glass in the icebox and the plate in your room or another safe place. Keep an accurate record of what you see happening. Use both words and pictures. Be patient. This experiment may take several days.

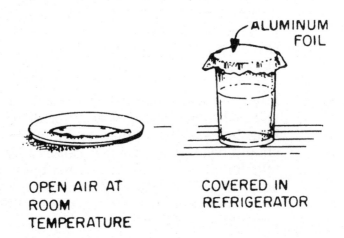

OPEN AIR AT ROOM TEMPERATURE

COVERED IN REFRIGERATOR

 Repeat the above experiment with sugar. Then repeat it with baking soda. What differences do you notice between the salt, sugar, and baking soda experiments? Make a list of all these differences. What do your observations tell you about how salt, sugar, and baking soda dissolve and crystallize? The sugar experiment may take several weeks before you notice any changes. You can use a few tiny grains of sugar as seed crystals to help if crystals don't form in a week. A seed crystal is a small crystal of the substance you are trying to crystallize. When you put a seed crystal in a concentrated solution of the substance, the small bits in solution can start collecting on the surface of the seed crystal, and it will grow bigger.

 Fill one clear glass soup or cereal bowl with colorless regular soda and another with colorless diet soda (Sprite® or 7 Up®). Put them on a shelf where dust cannot fall into them, and keep a record of what happens over time. Be very patient. This experiment may also take several weeks.

 Dissolve a whole glass of sugar in a half a glass of very hot water (boiling hot water is best). **(If you use boiling water you must have a parent help you!)** The solution should be like syrup. Tie a small nail to one end of a piece of string, and the other end to the center of a pencil. Wind the string around the pencil until the distance to the nail is about half the distance from the top of the glass to the bottom. Wet the string and nail, and drag them through a pile of sugar to get sugar crystals to stick to them. Hang the nail and string in the cooled syrup by placing the pencil over the top of the glass.

 Put some aluminum foil loosely over the top and place the glass in a place where it won't be disturbed. Punch a few large holes in the aluminum foil. After several days, you should begin to see some crystals. How are the sugar crystals different from the experiment you did above with sugar on the plate? Are they the same shape and size? What is happening on the string? How is it different from what is happening on the plate?

ALUMINUM FOIL
COVER WITH HOLES

 You can try to make salt crystals using string and a nail, just like you made sugar crystals. Compare them to salt crystals you made on the plate.

 If you live near the ocean, get a gallon jug of sea water. With your parents help, boil it on a stove in a large pot until the water is reduced to about a half a quart. Let this cool and pour it out onto a clear glass plate. Keep a record of what happens over several weeks. Do you see anything familiar? Explain. You can repeat this experiment with water from the faucet to compare it with sea water.

 Start a crystal collection. You can begin with the crystals you made from salt and sugar. You can get more at a nature store, hobby shop, or at a rock and mineral show. You might also get a crystal growing kit at the hobby shop or nature store. Look for crystals when you take a hike.

 Draw pictures of as many different kinds of crystals as you can find. Label the pictures with the names of the substances if you can. Do different substances form crystals that look similar?

Questions to Write and Draw

 Get a quartz crystal from a hobby store and draw a picture of it. How might such a crystal form?

 Take two different pieces of quartz crystal. Make a list of all the things that are the same about the two crystals. Pay particular attention to the shapes and angles you see. Make a list of all the things that are different about the crystals. Take two different crystalline materials, like a quartz crystal and an iron pyrite crystal (fool's gold). Make a list of all the things that are the same about the two crystals. Pay particular attention to the shapes and angles you see. Make a list of all the things that are different about the crystals.

 How are crystals of salt and sugar different? How are they the same? Write a detailed description of how a crystal of salt can form in a solution of salt water. Draw pictures to go with your description.

 What is the opposite of crystallization? What are the conditions that make crystallization happen?

 Why do salt and sugar seem to disappear when they dissolve in water?

 How are dissolving and melting different?

 Make a list of all the things you know are crystals. What solid things are not crystals?

 Make a list of some solid things you can buy in the grocery store that will dissolve in water.

Next time you go to the grocery store, make a list of all the things you can buy which are crystalline. Write a paragraph which explains what you like about crystals.

For Parents and Teachers

Getting Started

Children are fascinated by crystals. An easy way to get them talking about the subject is to bring in a box of various kinds. These are easily obtained at rock shops or rock and mineral shows. Try to get crystals of different shapes and colors. Have each child take one, draw a picture of it, and write a description. Ask them where they have seen crystals in the natural world. Many of them will have seen quartz crystals before, and some may even have rock collections with crystalline minerals. Other examples you could mention would be snowflakes, frost, and ice freezing on the surface of a pond. Crystals from the grocery store include salt, sugar, rock salt, and rock candy. Instant coffee advertised as "coffee crystals" is not really crystalline material. Though the surface of these chunks is shiny, they are not composed of tiny bits in a regular array. A real crystalline substance has a repeating regular pattern of tiny bits throughout the crystal. Substances which do not have this crystalline pattern are called *amorphous.*

Ask how crystals might form. Collect the explanations on a blackboard, overhead, or piece of paper. Cooling liquids often crystallize and this observation may come up (the transformation of water to ice). If it doesn't, you can introduce it, with frost, snow, and freezing puddles as examples. Sometimes crystals form by evaporation of solutions. Children who have visited mineral springs or who have noticed the residue formed when ocean water evaporates may recall this.

At this point you can have samples of salt and sugar ready to examine under a magnifying glass. Differences between these crystals can be elaborated by writing and drawing exercises. If you have access to a high-power binocular microscope this would be very helpful. If not, good magnifying glasses are sufficient. You might also wish to purchase some clear rock candy or larger, coarse-grained salt from the grocery store.

Be patient in getting crystals to form by evaporation of solutions as described in the Experiments section, because it can take some time. Salt crystals will usually form within a week, but sugar crystals take quite a bit longer and can also form syrupy masses of crystal. You can speed up the process by adding a seed crystal. The solid which crystallizes out when diet soda is evaporated is, in large part, the sugar substitute aspartame (NutraSweet®).

A Deeper Look

Crystallization from a solution is the reverse of dissolving. You should review *A Deeper Look* in Chapter 3 before you read this section on crystallization. Crystallization can occur in several ways. The type of crystallization referred to in the conversation between Maria and her father is that which occurs from a solution of a solid in a liquid. The solid crystallizes out of the solution. Crystallization of a pure liquid to its corresponding pure solid is called freezing, and it's discussed in Chapter 7. It's the reverse of melting. An example of this latter kind of crystallization is the conversion of liquid water to ice.

One of the most common liquids from which dissolved solids deposit crystals is water. Crystallization of a solid from water is the reverse of dissolving the solid in water. Whether crystallization or dissolution occurs depends on the temperature and on how much water is present, relative to the solid material dissolving or crystallizing. In a solution of a solid in water the dissolved bits are far apart from each other, with water surrounding them. Because of this, the solid is not visible. During crystallization, the bits of dissolved solid come together to form a visible crystal.

Two common ways of causing crystals to form from a water solution of a dissolved solid are to: 1) lower the temperature of the solution (dissolved substances often are less soluble and will crystallize out of solution when the temperature is lowered), and 2) evaporate some of the water off so that the concentration of the solute increases.

In the dialogue between Maria and her father the effects of both 1) and 2) are combined so that salt readily crystallizes on the plate. The major effect is the second one, however. In addition, a plate is used so that the surface area of the solution is large. This speeds up the evaporation process facilitating crystal formation. You can do the experiment using a glass of salt water instead of pouring it on a plate. The crystals will be larger, but it may take several weeks before you see them. Putting in a string coated with seed salt crystals can help promote crystallization from the solution.

There are many different kinds of crystals. Two major types are crystals formed from positive and negative particles (ions) and crystals formed from neutral particles (molecules). Crystals of table salt (sodium chloride) are an example of the former. They are formed from positive sodium ions and negative chloride ions which come together in a three-dimensional lattice array which has a cubic form. The strong attractive force of the positive sodium ions for the negative chloride ions holds the crystal together.

This attractive force is electrical in nature. It is very much like the attractive force you feel when you hold a magnet and a piece of iron near each other. While this is an example of a magnetic force, not an electrical force, it is a useful experiential way of illustrating the nature of a force between particles. A common electrical force is that between a balloon which has acquired a charge so that it sticks to a wall. Though this is easy to see, it is much harder to feel than the magnetic force between a magnet and a piece of iron.

Two ways of representing a crystal of sodium chloride, common table salt

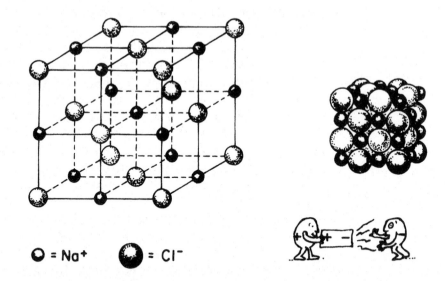

O = Na$^+$ ● = Cl$^-$

Sugar crystals are formed from neutral sugar particles (molecules). There are many different kinds of sugars. Two which are very important are *sucrose*, the chemical name for table sugar, and *glucose*, blood sugar. Sucrose is found in many fruits and vegetables. Large amounts are found in sugar beets and sugarcane. Glucose is found in honey and in some fruits. Glucose is also the breakdown product of starch. When we eat starchy foods and digest them, the digestion product is glucose.

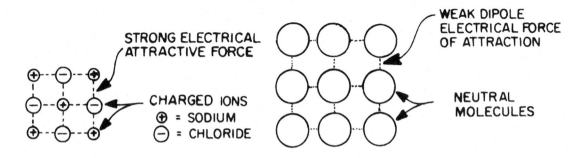

STRONG ELECTRICAL ATTRACTIVE FORCE

WEAK DIPOLE ELECTRICAL FORCE OF ATTRACTION

CHARGED IONS
⊕ = SODIUM
⊖ = CHLORIDE

NEUTRAL MOLECULES

The attractive forces which hold sugar molecules together in a sugar crystal are much weaker than those which hold sodium chloride together in a salt crystal. Much more sugar than salt will dissolve in a given amount of water, and sugar melts at a much lower temperature than salt (see Chapter 7).

There are a variety of different crystal forms. They occur because the sizes and attractive forces between various ions or molecules of different substances are different. A number of different crystal forms are shown below:

Some types of crystals

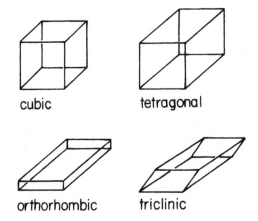

cubic   tetragonal

orthorhombic   triclinic

You may wish to purchase crystal models which show the individual ions or molecules in the crystal lattice. A catalogue is available from Klinger Educational Products Corporation, 112–19th Road, College Point, New York (Phone: 1–800–522–6252).

Putting Things Together

Mixing

" When you mix your money with someone else's money it's the end of your money. "

Diana: Mommy, what's pure?

Mother: What do you mean, pure?

D: On the carton of orange juice we bought it says "pure orange juice, a rich source of vitamin C." On the salad dressing bottle it says "made with pure sunflower oil, a rich source of polyunsaturates" and on the milk carton it says "pure milk, a rich source of vitamin D." And I don't know what pure means. Is it a rich source?

M: The word "pure" is put on the labels so people will buy those things. People believe that pure is good, as opposed to not pure. A rich source means there's a lot of whatever it is in there, vitamin C, D, or polyunsaturates.

D: Well isn't pure better than not pure? What's not pure? Do they sell things that aren't pure?

M: Actually, very few things are really pure. It depends on what you mean, and people are very confused about meanings. The confusion helps juice, salad dressing, and milk makers sell their products and make money though.

D: So what does pure mean?

M: It has different meanings. There are precise definitions which have to do with how many different things are mixed together, and then there are mushy definitions which have to do with what people think is good or bad.

D: I don't understand.

M: Take orange juice for example. What's it made of?

D: That's easy Mommy, it's made of oranges. You cut the orange in half and squeeze it and the juice comes out. I can make it myself.

M: But what's in the juice?

D: I don't *know!* Juice is juice. It's different from milk or root beer.

M: How is it different?

D: It's colored orange. Is that why it's called orange juice? Because it comes from oranges? Or do they call the fruit orange because it's colored orange? Which came first, the color or the fruit?

M: You're getting off the track, aren't you? What about pure and not pure? I asked you what's in the juice.

D: I don't know what's in it. That's why I got off the track; I don't like it when you ask me things I don't know.

M: OK. There's water in it.

D: Well, I know that, Mommy. They have to water the orange trees and the water goes into the tree and oranges. But it tastes better than water.

M: So it has water in it, but it's different than water. How is it different?

D: It's sweeter and lumpier, and I can't see through it like water.

M: What might make it sweet?

D: Sugar?

M: Yes, I think so. And why can't you see through it?

D: Because it's so orange. And it's filled with orange lumps.

M: What's the orange color from?

D: You tell me Mommy. I don't know.

M: It's a reddish-yellow pigment.

D: Pigment?! From pigs. How could pigs get into . . .?

M: Wait. Let's just call it reddish-yellow bits, not pigs or pigments.

D: Is that all? Water, sugar, and reddish-yellow bits?

M: No. It's got other things as well. There's citric acid and ascorbic acid and . . . .

D: Mommy . . . *stop!* I won't want to drink my juice with all those things in it.

M: Precisely.

D: What?

M: Calling something "pure" makes people want to buy it. It makes you want to drink orange juice when I call it pure, doesn't it?

D: Yes, it does. So my orange juice isn't really pure, but it's OK to drink it?

M: Of course!

D: I thought pure was simple. Pure orange juice is just one thing, orange juice!

M: Well, that's true. But that meaning is the mushy meaning, and it's sometimes misused by people selling juice, and soap, and oil in order to get people to buy their products. Let's try to make a better meaning.

D: Like what?

M: Let's call something pure when it's a single thing, not a mixture. Orange juice is a mixture of water, sugar, vitamins, and other things. So it isn't really pure by my definition.

D: So something is really pure when it's a single thing, not a mixture? Then my orange juice isn't pure because it has lots of stuff in it!

M: Exactly.

D: Then they shouldn't put "pure" on the label.

M: But their meaning isn't the same. They just mean that they didn't put artificial color in it, or artificial flavors, and that it isn't contaminated.

D: I guess that's OK then. As long as I understand. Is my orange juice pure?

M: Do you mean uncontaminated?

D: I don't know, do I?

M: Yes, I hope so. You don't want to drink contaminated juice. It wouldn't be contaminated unless there was a terrible mistake at the juice factory. Something that is contaminated has undesirable things mixed into it that make it harmful.

D: But it isn't pure?

M: It isn't a single thing, but it's OK to drink it. It is nice to be clear about things sometimes isn't it?

D: If you say so—but—it isn't really that clear to me! Is water a pure thing?

M: Yes, if it doesn't have anything in it.

D: Oh good. We finally have a *really pure* thing. Water is just water. It's not mixed with anything else. And if it's not contaminated, it's pure *both ways* isn't it?

M: Yes. There are two kinds of things in the world, pure things and mixtures. And the mixtures are just two or more of the pure things mixed up. Most things are mixtures, like orange juice, salad dressing, and milk. Even vegetable oil is a mixture.

D: So how do I know the difference between a mixture and a real pure thing?

M: Well, it isn't that easy to tell sometimes. For example, if I showed you a glass of water it would be hard for you to tell if it was pure water or whether I had dissolved a bit of sugar in it.

D: But I could Mommy, I could. I would just taste it and I would know which was the mixture.

M: That's true . . . you could. But sometimes it wouldn't be as easy.

D: So how can you always tell the difference?

M: Even though it's sometimes hard to do, you can always physically separate a mixture into its component parts. You can distill it, or filter it, or do other things to it, and get the components apart. If you have a pure substance you can't do that because you have only one thing.

D: Are there any really pure things besides water?

M: There are lots of pure things. Sugar for example. The sugar in the grocery store is a remarkably pure thing. And aluminum foil is pure aluminum. Many metals are pure things, like copper wire. Baking soda is also pure and so is a diamond. None of those things are mixed with other things.

D: But most things in the grocery store are mixtures aren't they?

M: Yes, most things are, like juices, milk, soda, and wine. And other foods like bread, cereal, meats, vegetables, ice cream, and soup are also mixtures.

D: When I make Kool-Aid® I make a mixture don't I?

M: Yes, you do. You mix pure water with Kool-Aid® powder, which is already a mixture of sugar, coloring, and flavors.

D: If I mix water with just sugar then am I taking two pure things and making a mixture? It's a solution of sugar in water. So solutions of a solid in a liquid must be mixtures. Isn't that so?

M: Yes, it is. All pure things are either *elements*, like iron, copper, and carbon, or *compounds*, like sugar, salt, and water.

You can mix elements with elements, or compounds with compounds, or elements with compounds. And in all those cases you get mixtures.

D: It seems very complicated.

M: It can be if you don't get it clear in your head. It helps to write it down. There are only two kinds of pure things, elements and compounds. The trouble is that it takes time to learn which is which. Once you know that, the rest is a little easier. When you mix pure things together you always get a mixture.

D: I think I understand, Mommy. Like now I have two different thoughts in my head at the same time. Is that what happens when I get mixed up?

M: That's interesting. Yes! A mixture of thoughts seems similar to a mixture of things doesn't it? That's probably what we mean when we say we're confused . . . mixed up!

D: And I'm a mixture too, aren't I? My bones, skin, and muscles are kind of all mixed together.

M: Yes, you are a mixture of water, proteins, fats, oils, vitamins, and. . . .

D: But . . . I don't feel mixed up!

M: Now you're mixing meanings about feelings and things.

D: I am? Aren't feelings things?

M: Oh Diana, enough. Let's go shopping.

D: Ok. And I want to read the labels to find the pure things and the mixtures. I'm going to tell the manager when I find a mixture that says pure on the label.

M: That should be very interesting. Mind if I listen in on your conversation?

D: Nope. Let's go!

Mixing–A Description

Mixing occurs when two pure things are combined together. Dissolving sugar in water, which we have already considered in Chapter 3, is an example of a mixture. In this instance, water, a pure substance, is mixed with sugar, a pure substance. The resulting mixture is a solution of sugar in water which looks like plain water, but it isn't. It's a mixture in which water and sugar bits are all mixed up.

A mixture of this type is called *homogeneous,* which means it is the same throughout. A mixture of oil and water is called *heterogeneous* because the oil bits and water bits do not mix. The oil sits on top of the water. Mixtures in which you can *see* the individual components are always called heterogeneous. If you can't see the components, the mixture is homogeneous.

There are two kinds of pure substances, elements and compounds. Neither of these can be physically separated into simpler components. Examples of elements are carbon, a black solid, and sulfur, a yellow solid. Some elements, like mercury, are liquid, whereas others, like oxygen, are colorless gases. The symbols for elements are often the first letters of the name of the element (i.e., C for carbon and S for sulfur). The periodic table, shown on the following page, is a chart of all the elements.

Compounds are pure substances that contain two or more elements *chemically combined* together in a fixed ratio. The elements no longer have their elemental properties when chemically combined in a compound: They share or trade parts of themselves and change into something different. A compound is not just a mixture of two elements. It is a new pure substance, made of molecules or ions (see the Glossary for how *ions* form from elements). The elements which make up a compound cannot be physically separated from the compound which they make. The properties of the pure compound are entirely different from the elements which combined to form it. You will learn about chemical combination in Chapter 9. Some examples of different com-

94

A simplified periodic table of the elements (heavy line divides the metals from the nonmetals)

Metals					Nonmetals					Noble Gases
Group IA	Group IIA	A few transition metals			Group IIIA	Group IVA	Group VA	Group VIA	Group VIIA	Group VIIIA
H Hydrogen										He Helium
Li Lithium					B Boron	C Carbon	N Nitrogen	O Oxygen	F Fluorine	Ne Neon
Na Sodium	Mg Magnesium				Al Aluminum	Si Silicon	P Phosphorus	S Sulfur	Cl Chlorine	Ar Argon
K Potassium	Ca Calcium	Fe Iron	Cu Copper	Zu Zinc	Ga Gallium	Ge Germanium	As Arsenic	Se Selenium	Br Bromine	Kr Krypton
Rb Rubidium	Sr Strontium		Ag Silver	Cd Cadmium	IN Indium	Sn Tin	Sb Antimony	Te Tellurium	I Iodine	Xe Xenon
Cs Cesium	Ba Barium		Au Gold	Hg Mercury	Th Thallium	Pb Lead	Bi Bismuth	Po Polonium	At Astatine	Rn Radon

pounds formed from two different elements are shown below which illustrate the concepts just discussed.

The compound water is composed of the element hydrogen and the element oxygen. Hydrogen is a colorless gas which rapidly reacts with the oxygen in air when a spark or

H_2O

$NaCl$

WATER, A MOLECULAR COMPOUND FORMED FROM THE ELEMENTS HYDROGEN O AND OXYGEN ● (H AND O) IN A RATIO OF TWO TO ONE.

SALT, AN IONIC COMPOUND FORMED FROM THE ELEMENTS SODIUM AND CHLORINE AS THEIR IONS (Na^+ = O ; Cl^- = ●)

flame ignites the mixture. Oxygen is also a colorless gas. The chemical reaction of hydrogen and oxygen produces water. This is the same reaction that occurs when hydrogen and oxygen are burned as fuel to launch the space shuttle. A mixture of hydrogen and oxygen that has not reacted is just a mixture of colorless gases. This mixture can be separated physically. Water cannot be physically separated into its elements. It no longer has the properties of its reactants, hydrogen and oxygen. It is a new pure compound, not a mixture of hydrogen and oxygen.

Common table salt is formed from the elements sodium, a silver-colored, very reactive, and hazardous metal, and chlorine, a very poisonous, greenish-yellow gas. Salt is a normal component of our blood, but sodium metal and chlorine gas are so poisonous that if we were to touch them, they would damage our fingers.

Sugar is composed of the elements carbon, hydrogen, and oxygen, a black solid and two colorless gases. It is not a mixture of these elements. So you can see that compounds are not just mixtures of elements. They are chemically combined elements. A mixture of carbon, hydrogen, and oxygen in a jar would just look like a black substance under colorless invisible gases. When chemically combined, the white crystalline solid, sugar, results. This solid has none of the properties of the elements carbon, hydrogen, and oxygen (see *physical properties* and *chemical properties* in the Glossary).

All mixtures are combinations of pure substances (elements and compounds). One can have 1) a mixture of different elements, 2) a mixture of elements and compounds, or 3) a mixture of compounds. Consider the *elements* sodium, chlorine, and fluorine. Let's pretend that a red gumdrop is like the element sodium, a green gumdrop is like the element chlorine, and a yellow gumdrop is like the element fluorine.

We can also pretend that the *compound* sodium chloride, common table salt, is like a toothpick with a red gumdrop on one end and a green gumdrop on the other end. And we can pretend that the *compound* sodium fluoride, used in toothpaste to help prevent tooth decay, is a toothpick with a red gumdrop on one end and a yellow gumdrop on the other end.

> red gumdrop = *element* sodium
> green gumdrop = *element* chlorine
> yellow gumdrop = *element* fluorine
> red and green gumdrop on a toothpick = *compound* sodium chloride
> red and yellow gumdrop on a toothpick = *compound* sodium fluoride

We can then make three different kinds of mixtures:

1. *A mixture of different elements*: a mixture of *green and yellow gumdrops* (i.e., a mixture of chlorine and fluorine).

2. *A mixture of an element and a compound:* a mixture of green gumdrops with toothpicks having a red gumdrop on one end and a green one on the other end (i.e., a mixture of chlorine and sodium chloride).

3. *A mixture of different compounds:* a mixture of toothpicks having a red gumdrop on one end and a green one on the other, with toothpicks having a red gumdrop on one end and a yellow on the other (i.e., a mixture of sodium chloride and sodium fluoride).

GREEN AND YELLOW GUMDROPS:
A MIXTURE OF ELEMENTS
Y   AND   G

GREEN GUMDROPS AND
TOOTHPICK WITH RED
GUMDROP ON ONE END,
GREEN ON THE OTHER:
MIXTURE OF ELEMENT
AND COMPOUND   G
G   R

RED AND GREEN GUMDROPS ON A
TOOTHPICK MIXED WITH RED AND
YELLOW GUMDROPS ON A TOOTHPICK:
MIXTURE OF COMPOUND
WITH COMPOUND   Y   G
R   G

Most things in the world are mixtures. Because elements and compounds can be solids, liquids, or gases, there are many different kinds of mixtures. You can mix a solid with a solid, like salt and sugar. You can mix a liquid with a liquid, like water and alcohol. Or you can mix a solid with a liquid, like a solution of salt in water. You can also mix a gas with a liquid. An example of this kind of mixture is soda water. You don't see the gas in the liquid until you take off the cap and allow the gas to escape.

Whether a mixture is homogeneous (the same throughout) or heterogeneous (different in different parts of the mixture) depends upon how big the pieces of the various components of the mixture are. It can be easy to separate the components of such a mixture. For example, you could easily separate the components of a mixture of marbles and raisins just by picking them apart. You'd have a much harder time separating a mixture of flour and powdered sugar. We'll talk more about separating things in Chapter 6.

Mixing

pure substance A   pure substance B   mixing   mixture of A and B

Experiments

 Take five glasses of water, each about ¾ full, and label them 1 through 5 by taping a small piece of paper on each. Add a tablespoon of salt to glass 1, a tablespoon of sand to glass 2, a tablespoon of flour to glass 3, a tablespoon of vegetable oil to glass 4, and a tablespoon of apple juice to glass 5. Stir the mixture in each glass for a minute or so. Describe the mixtures you have made and draw pictures to accompany your descriptions. Which mixtures are homogeneous? Which are heterogeneous?

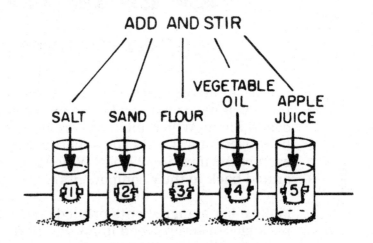

5 GLASSES OF WATER

 Try the above experiment using vegetable oil instead of water in the five glasses. In glass 4 add a tablespoon of water, not a tablespoon of vegetable oil. What differences in the five mixtures do you notice compared to the first experiment with water in the five glasses?

 Take five glasses and label them 1 through 5. Add two table-spoons of sugar to each. Then add a tablespoon of salt to glass 1, a tablespoon of flour to glass 2, a tablespoon of cloves to glass 3, a tablespoon of raisins to glass 4, and a tablespoon of sand to glass 5.

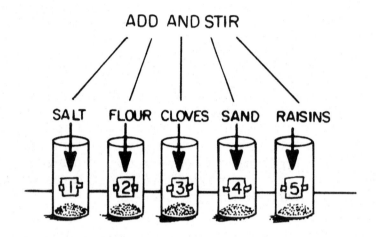

ADD AND STIR

SALT FLOUR CLOVES SAND RAISINS

5 GLASSES CONTAINING SUGAR

 Stir each mixture with a clean dry spoon. Describe the mix-tures you have made and draw pictures to accompany your descriptions. Which mixtures are homogeneous? Which are heterogeneous? Could you separate the ingredients from each of the mixtures? How? Which mixtures cannot be sep-arated back to their components?

 Make a list of ingredients printed on the side or back of packages of several food items you find in your refrigerator or in your kitchen cabinets. Then read the front of the labels to see how the manufacturer describes the product. What ingredients do you recognize? Do some of the products have the same ingredients? Can you see the individual ingredi-ents in some of the food items? Which food items are homo-geneous mixtures? Which are heterogeneous? Can you separate any of the components from a product into a separate pile?

 With your parents help, try making some experimental mixtures using food items from the kitchen. For example you might mix ketchup with vinegar, ice cream with mustard, or milk with lemon juice. Write careful descriptions of your mixtures. Ask your parents to help you think up new mixtures. Don't forget to have an adult help you, and to clean up after you do the experiment. Mix *only* edible food items.

 Next time you go to the supermarket, examine several products. Take a notebook and copy the descriptions shown on the front labels of these products and see how they compare to the list of ingredients in small print on the side or back of the labels. Do you know the meaning of the units listed for the amounts of ingredients? If not, ask and find out.

 Make a list of all the pure elements you can find in the grocery and hardware store. Make a list of some pure compounds you find in these stores. If you don't know whether something is an element or compound, ask your teacher or parents, or look it up in a dictionary. Is it easy to tell if you have an element or compound? Is it easy to tell if your elements and compounds are pure?

Questions to Write and Draw

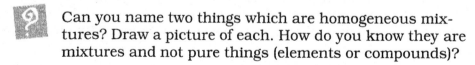

? Can you name two things which are homogeneous mixtures? Draw a picture of each. How do you know they are mixtures and not pure things (elements or compounds)?

? Describe how a homogeneous mixture is different from a heterogeneous mixture. Draw a picture to illustrate your description.

? Describe different ways of making mixtures.

? If water is composed of small bits and alcohol is composed of small bits, describe how a homogeneous solution of alcohol and water is formed. In your description, consider the positions and movements of the small bits.

? Can you give examples of solid-solid mixtures? How about solid-liquid mixtures? How about gas-liquid mixtures? Draw a picture of each kind of mixture. Draw a picture of each kind of mixture using small bits to represent the components of the mixtures.

? What does the word "pure" mean? Make a list of pure substances.

? What does the word "contaminated" mean? Give an example.

? Look up definitions of the words *pure*, *mixture*, and *contaminated* in the dictionary. Write them out on separate sheets of paper. Can you put these definitions in your own words? Could you illustrate these definitions with pictures?

Explain to someone else how a product in the grocery store which has "pure" written on the label can have a whole list of ingredients.

 What kinds of kitchen appliances are used to make mixtures? How do they do this? What kinds of kitchen devices or appliances are used to separate mixtures? How do they do this?

For Parents and Teachers

Getting Started

Children have great fun preparing mixtures. Start out by having them make mixtures that are homogeneous, like solutions of salt in water, sugar in water, or Kool-Aid® powder in water. Review the material on dissolving in Chapter 3 before you begin. Re-emphasize that solutions are homogeneous mixtures because they look the same throughout. Then have them make mixtures using solids like raisins, peanuts, M & M's®, small gumdrops, cashews, or other things you may find convenient. You could also use tacks, nails, paper clips, buttons, etc., but *do not mix food items with non-food items*. Point out that all these mixtures are heterogeneous. They are not the same throughout. You can see the individual components in a heterogeneous mixture. You cannot see them in a homogeneous mixture.

Have children write descriptions of their mixtures and draw pictures to accompany the descriptions. Have them create their own kinds of mixtures and write descriptions using both words and pictures. Note that a mixture can have many different individual components, not just two. A mixture with only two components is called a binary mixture. Have them read food labels so they can see that what appears to be a single thing, like juice, milk, mayonnaise, ice cream, or other food items, are actually complex mixtures.

One interesting mixture they can make is vegetable oil and water, a heterogeneous liquid mixture which forms two layers. This can be done in a Mason jar. The lid can be screwed on tightly and the mixture can be shaken. The children can then watch it separate out into two layers. This can be contrasted with a mixture of syrup in water which initially forms layers, but which will turn homogeneous upon shaking or stirring. The individual components (the water and syrup) cannot be identified individually after mixing.

HETEROGENEOUS   HOMOGENEOUS
MIXTURE   MIXTURE

Other interesting things children like to mix are different colored waxes. Differently colored crayons or waxes can be melted and mixed together. These experiments are a bit more involved than making simple mixtures that do not require heating the components. The wax or crayons can usually be melted by placing them in a can sitting in very hot water. Do not heat wax or crayons directly on a flame or hot plate as they can burn!

Use your imagination in creating new mixing experiments. Try them yourself before you have the children do them. *Avoid hazardous or toxic materials* like paints, garden products, or harsh cleaning products like washing powder,

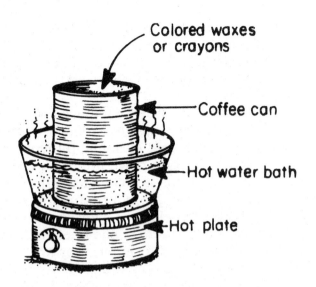

Colored waxes or crayons

Coffee can

Hot water bath

Hot plate

Chlorox® or Drano®. **Read the labels for warnings!** You should also be aware that mixing certain products can result in a potentially dangerous chemical reaction (Chlorox® and ammonia or Drano® and water for example). Most food items can be safely mixed, so it is best to use them. The mixtures might be quite unappetizing (e.g., mustard and chocolate ice cream!), but they are safe. Reactions of common food ingredients, like vinegar and baking soda, are discussed in Chapter 9.

A Deeper Look

As noted previously in the dialogue and children's description, there are only two kinds of pure substances, *elements* and *compounds.* Elements are substances that cannot be broken down chemically into simpler substances. Aluminum, iron, sulfur, and carbon are examples of elements. Elements can be classified into two general types: metals and nonmetals. Aluminum and iron are metals. Carbon and sulfur are nonmetals. The chemical formula for an element is the letter symbol for that element, which may reflect an English, Latin, or other source name. The symbol for iron is Fe from the Latin *ferrum.* The symbol for sulfur is S. Neither iron nor sulfur can be broken down into simpler components. The letter symbols for all the elements can be found in the the *periodic table,* a listing which places elements in categories of similar properties. The periodic table of the elements is shown in the children's description of mixing.

Compounds are composed of chemically combined elements in fixed weight ratios (see the definition of *compound* in the glossary). Although difficult to do, compounds can always be broken down into their component elements. This decomposition is a chemical change, not a physical separation. An example of a compound is water, which is composed of the element hydrogen and the element oxygen in a fixed weight ratio of one to eight. The elements in water are not just mixed together, they are chemically combined. Hydrogen and oxygen are gases at room temperature and pressure, whereas water is a liquid. The properties of water are not at all like the properties of the hydrogen and oxygen which react to make it. The chemical formula for water is H_2O. Water contains two atoms of hydrogen and one atom of oxygen. Since an oxygen atom is sixteen times as heavy as a hydrogen atom, the weight of oxygen in water is eight times that of hydrogen. Water can be decomposed into its elements by electrolysis, a chemical process that can take place in a car battery under certain conditions. This chemical reaction requires considerable energy.

Another example of a compound is sugar. Table sugar is sucrose. It is composed of the elements carbon, C, hydrogen, H, and oxygen, O. Its chemical formula is $C_{12}H_{22}O_{11}$. Carbon is a black solid, and hydrogen and oxygen are colorless gases, but when these elements are chemically combined in sugar, the result is a sweet, white, solid. Sugar is a pure substance and cannot be physically separated into its elemental components. To get the elements back from sugar it must be chemically decomposed.

If two pure substances are mixed together mechanically, but do not react chemically, a simple binary mixture is obtained. For example, one can mix the element copper, Cu, a reddish metal, with the element sulfur, S, a yellow nonmetal. The result is a binary mixture. If the mixed elements were both powders, the resultant mixture would be difficult to separate into its components. However, if the copper and sulfur in the mixture were in the form of large pieces of each element (i.e., chunks of copper and sulfur) they could be separated simply by picking them apart manually. If the copper-sulfur mixture is heated, a chemical reaction occurs which yields copper sulfide, a new compound. Copper sulfide is not a mixture of copper and sulfur. It is a new compound formed by a chemical reaction of copper and sulfur. It has the formula CuS. This reaction is discussed in detail in Chapter 9. Though it can be done chemically, it is difficult to get the copper and sulfur back.

Mixtures can be made from elements like copper and sulfur, or from elements and compounds, like sulfur and sugar, or from compounds, like sugar and copper sulfide. A mixture can have an unlimited number of components. One can mix solids with solids, liquids with liquids, or liquids with solids. One can also mix gases with gases and gases with liquids. Mixtures of gases with solids are less common.

A diagram showing the relationship between elements, compounds, and different types of mixtures is shown on the next page. You will find it useful in discussing mixtures with children.

MATTER

PURE SUBSTANCES
salt, water, sugar, iron

Fixed Composition
Cannot be separated into simpler substances by physical methods.

MIXTURES
saltwater, bronze, pizza, air

Variable Composition
Can be separated into pure substances using physical methods (i.e. saltwater -> salt and water bronze -> copper and tin)

ELEMENT

A substance consisting of atoms of only one kind. i.e., gold, carbon, iron, sulfur.

Fe   Au

COMPOUND

A substance containing two or more elements chemically combined in a fixed ratio (i.e., salt contains sodium and chlorine; water contains hydrogen and oxygen.)

HOMO-GENEOUS MIXTURE

A mixture which has the same composition throughout, i.e., saltwater (salt dissolved in water), air (a mixture of nitrogen, oxygen and other gases).

HETERO-GENEOUS MIXTURE

A mixture which does not have the same composition throughout, i.e. pizza, granite, Trailmix.

Taking Things Apart
Separating

"When lightning separates from a cloud it can be quite shocking."

Jose: Daddy, Daddy, my *J* made a rainbow.

Father: What are you talking about, Jose?

J: I wrote my name on a piece of paper with a black marking pen and it got wet on the kitchen counter. And where it got wet on the *J* of my name it made a rainbow! Look. There's blue and red and brown. How does it happen?

F: Well, when you mix colors together, like blue and red and brown, they must make black. Why don't you try it with your paint set.

J: Oĸ. I will.

[later]

J: You're right, Daddy. When I mix blue, red, and brown I get black. I didn't know that would happen. It must be how they make black at the paint factory.

F: It's probably one way they can do it, Jose.

J: So why did the black turn back into blue, red, and brown when the *J* of my name got wet?

F: It didn't change into those colors, did it?

J: Yes, it did so!

110

F: But didn't it just get unmixed?

J: Unmixed? What does unmixed mean?

F: Separated. Didn't the colors that make up black separate on the wet paper?

J: What does separate mean?

F: Separate means to come apart. The black came apart into the colors that make it. It's the opposite of mixing.

J: Well—OK. But,—why did they do that? Just because the black *J* got wet, it came apart?

F: Let's try it again. Make a tiny dot of black with your marking pen on the bottom of a strip of paper. Let's cut a strip from the coffee filter paper in the kitchen. We'll tape the top of the strip to a pencil and hang it into a glass with a bit of water in the bottom so the paper just touches the water. Then we'll watch as the water goes up the paper.

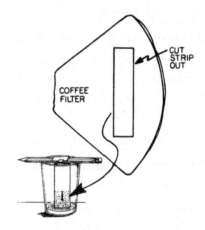

J: The water is going up the paper. It's crawling up.

F: What else?

J: When it comes to the black dot it smooshes it out.

F: Smooshes?

111

J: It's getting all blurry—and then . . .

F: What?

J: The colors start coming.

F: From where?

J: From the black spot!

F: So the water separates the colors. When they're mixed together they're black, but when the water goes through the spot they come out, one after another.

J: Yes, I see that. They come apart. Blue is on the top. Then the red comes. The last one is brown.

F: They separate.

J: Why? Why do they do that?

F: Well, the colors are really a large collection of very tiny bits. There are blue bits and red bits and brown bits. When all the bits are mixed up the colors combine to make the mixture look black.

J: So how does water make them come apart on the paper?

F: When you put the black spot on the paper, the blue, red, and brown bits stick to it all at the same place, right where you made the spot. And it looks black because the different bits are all together.

J: But what makes them separate when the water goes by?

F: I'm getting to that. Which color moves away from the black ink spot first?

J: Blue.

F: Oκ. Then it must be that the red and brown bits stick harder to the paper than the blue bits. The water washes away the blue first.

J: The red bits move more slowly. Why do they? Why do the red bits move more slowly than the blue bits? And why are the brown bits the slowest?

F: Because the brown bits like the paper much more than the red bits. They stick harder to it because they like it more than the water. The red bits like the water more, so they move with it and come away from the spot slowly. The blue bits like the water the best, so they move the fastest.

J: But why, Daddy? Why do the brown bits like the paper more and the blue bits like the water more? Why is that?

F: The brown bits are more like the paper and the blue bits are more like the water. The red bits are in between. Things that are like each other tend to stick together.

What's most important I think, is that you've discovered a way to separate the colors that make up black. You made a really interesting observation. Not everyone would have noticed those colors separating like you did.

J: Are there other ways of separating things?

F: Oh yes, lots of ways.

J: What?

F: You can name one yourself.

J: No I can't.

F: Yes, you can. Think for a moment about M & M's®. You're always separating out the green, red, and yellow M & M's® into piles before you eat them aren't you?

J: Oh Daddy, that's not the same at all.

F: Not exactly the same, but it's similar, isn't it. You're separating a mixture into its parts. The bits, the M & M's®, are just bigger than the color bits in the black ink, so you can see each of them and pick them apart with your fingers.

What if I gave you a mixture of salt and sand? Could you separate that into separate piles?

J: The grains are much too small. And some sand grains are white just like salt.

F: Yes, that's true. You couldn't do it by picking them apart with your hands, but could there be another way. Could you use water?

J: How?

F: What does salt do in water? Does it do the same thing as sand?

J: Salt dissolves in water, but sand doesn't because its all over the beach and the beach doesn't wash away.

F: That's true.

J: So I could pour the mixture of salt and sand into a glass of water and stir it up.

F: What would happen?

J: The salt would dissolve, and then I could pour off the water with the salt in it. Only sand would be left.

F: You could pour it through a coffee filter that we use to pour hot water through coffee.

J: That's a good idea. The filter would catch the sand.

F: And what about the salt?

J: It would be in the water.

F: How could you get it back?

J: I don't know!

F: Yes you do.

J: I *don't*.

F: What about evaporation and crystallization? Remember Maria told you she grew salt crystals from water?

J: Oh, I remember! If I pour the salt water on a plate and let the water evaporate I'll get the salt back as crystals.

F: Good idea, Jose.

J: Daddy?

F: Yes?

J: How would I get a mixture of salt and sugar apart? They both dissolve in water and they're both white.

F: You'll have to try some experiments.

J: I guess I will. I like experiments.

F: Just tell me what you plan to do first, OK?

J: Sure Daddy. I wonder how I could separate flour, powdered sugar, and hot chocolate mix?

F: Keep it simple Jose, OK? You're making things too complicated.

J: How about ketchup, milk, soda, and cherry syrup?

F: Enough, Jose!

Separating–A Description

In Chapter 5 you learned about mixing and various types of mixtures. Mixtures can be taken apart into their components. A simple example is separating money. If you have three dollars worth of pennies, nickels, and dimes, you can separate each type of coin into its own pile. This is easy because pennies, nickels, and dimes are all different, and they are large enough to pick apart by hand. You can do the same thing with a pile of colored M & M's®, separating them into piles of red, green, yellow, and brown.

Separating a mixture is harder if the components of the mixture are smaller, and if there are large numbers of them. For example, if you had a mixture of peanuts, raisins, tiny marshmallows, popcorn, gumdrops, corn chips, and almonds, it would take you longer to separate them into piles of each component. It would take even longer to separate a mixture of uncooked brown and white rice.

The above mixtures can be separated by hand. If the component parts of the mixture are very small, this way of separating them from each other isn't easy. For example, if you had a mixture of salt and sand it would be very difficult to separate it by picking the pieces apart. The grains of salt and sand are too small. In addition, some sand grains are white and look very much like grains of salt. There are other ways of separating sand from salt that depend upon the ways that sand and salt are different.

Salt dissolves in water to form a solution. Sand does not dissolve in water. If you add it to a glass of water, it just sinks to the bottom. So if you add a mixture of salt and sand to water, the salt will dissolve and the sand won't. Now, how can you get the sand away from the solution of salt in water, and how can you get the salt back?

A good way of separating a liquid from a solid (the salt water solution from the sand) is to filter it. To filter something means to pour it through a paper or *filter* which lets the liquid part through but stops the solid part. If you stir the mixture up and then pour it through a coffee filter, the salt water solution will go through the filter and the sand will not. You can then let the sand dry. If you put the salt water solution on a clear glass plate and let the water evaporate, you can get the salt back. This is an example of crystallization which we discussed in Chapter 4.

While the process of filtration can be used to separate a solid from a liquid, the process of evaporation, described in Chapter 1, can be used to separate a liquid from a dissolved solid. There are other methods which can be used to separate components of a mixture. Some of these are too complicated to describe in detail, but you might wish to read about them on your own. One very common method for separating complex mixtures is called *chromatography*. There are many different kinds of chromatography. The simplest is paper chromatography.

An example of paper chromatography is described in the conversation between Jose and his father. Paper chromatography works best for separating a mixture of colored substances, because the colors allow the separation to be seen. While this method doesn't allow the separation of a large amount of a mixture into piles of components, it does reveal that some substances, which we might have thought were only a single thing, are in fact mixtures. And when the components of a mixture are very tiny bits, it is one of the best ways of getting them apart.

Black ink is a mixture of several colors. Each color is composed of tiny bits of a particular color type. When all the bits are mixed together, their individual colors don't show.

Instead the mixture looks black. If you put a spot of black ink near the bottom of a strip of absorbent paper (a strip of coffee filter paper works best), and put the very bottom of the strip in water, the water will travel up the paper towards the spot of black ink. As it passes the black spot, the colored bits in the black ink that are most attracted to the water will begin to follow it up the paper. The colored bits that are less attracted to the water will follow less rapidly, and as the water moves farther and farther along the paper, the colored bits from the ink will separate into bands of color. Each band contains a large collection of a particular kind of colored bit. This separation is called chromatography (colors—drawn out).

Separating

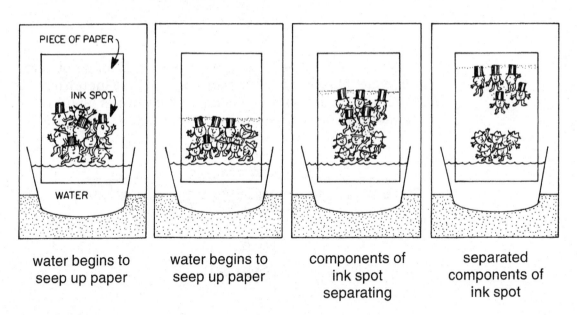

PIECE OF PAPER
INK SPOT
WATER

| water begins to seep up paper | water begins to seep up paper | components of ink spot separating | separated components of ink spot |

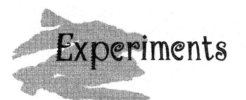

Experiments

 Cut a strip of coffee filter paper about 4 inches long and ¾ of an inch wide. Make a tiny ink spot about a half-inch from the bottom of the paper strip using a black, water-soluble, felt-tip marking pen. Tape the top of the paper strip to the

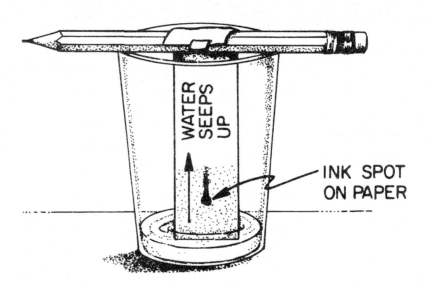

WATER SEEPS UP

INK SPOT
ON PAPER

118

side of a pencil and hang it in a glass so that the bottom of the strip is about an inch from the bottom of the glass. Add a little over an inch of water to the bottom of a glass so that the paper below the ink spot touches the water. What do you notice as the water seeps up the paper?

 Try the above experiment using brown, red, green, and purple water-soluble felt-tip marking pens. What differences do you notice?

 Let the strips dry. Do they look different when they are wet and dry? After they dry, draw a border around each separate color on the strips with a pencil. Label the colors. What colors make up brown ink? What colors make up black ink?

 Try this experiment using some rubbing alcohol instead of water in the glass. Are the results different? Why? Try it with vegetable oil. Does it work? Why not?

 Propose a method that would allow you to separate the following mixtures: 1. peanuts, gum drops, and raisins; 2. paper clips, salt, and pennies; 3. salt, sand, and sawdust; 4. iron filings, aluminum filings, and sugar; 5. salt, iron filings, and cinnamon powder. Try out one of your methods to see if it works. Redesign your separation method based on the results of your trial.

 Using a coffee filter and some clear plastic glasses, see if you can find a way of separating the components of an oil and vinegar salad dressing which has spices and seasonings floating in it. **Get permission,** do this in the kitchen, and clean up your mess after you are finished.

 With your parent's help and permission, get some different mesh screens from the hardware store. With help, build a small frame for the screens and use them to screen rocks and soil in your backyard. Can you separate out different size components from the soil into different piles? What do the piles look like? Describe each one.

 Using a binocular microscope, examine some of the products from the grocery store that are mixtures (powdered spice mixtures, drink mixes, cake mixes, cereal mixtures, etc.). Write down descriptions of each component that you can see. Count the number of components in each product. Estimate the amount of each component in each product. Are there ways you might separate some of the components from these products?

 Try this again using sand. Try it using some soil from your backyard. After you have carefully examined the soil and written a description of the components, add it to a glass of water and stir it for a minute or two. After it stands for twenty minutes, pour off the liquid into another glass. Let the remaining solid dry, and let the water in the second glass evaporate off (this will take some time). Examine the two different residues with a binocular microscope. Compare them with the original soil. Write down a description of the residues noting the differences from the original soil.

Questions to Write and Draw

 Draw a diagram and write an explanation of how water seeping up a strip of filter paper past a black ink spot can separate the ink into its component colors.

 Write a description of how you can recover the salt from a solution of salt dissolved in water. Can you think of a way to recover the water?

 Write a list of all the different ways you can think of to separate mixtures. Use pictures and diagrams where necessary.

 Using a description of water and alcohol as different kinds of small bits, describe how a homogeneous solution (mixture) of alcohol and water can be separated using the process of distillation. In your description, consider the positions and movements of the small bits during the distillation process. Diagrams would be helpful. You may have to do some research on distillation in the library and read part of Chapter 8 to do this.

 Illustrate how you would separate: 1) a mixture of large pieces of two different solids which are both insoluble; 2) an insoluble solid mixed in a liquid; 3) a mixture of a gas dissolved in a liquid; and 4) a mixture of two different liquids which do not mix with each other (one floats on top of the other).

 Describe the meaning of each of the following terms: *chromatography*, *filtration*, and *distillation*.

 How would screens or sieves of different sized "holes" be useful in separating mixtures of solids of different sizes?

Which do you think are easiest to separate, homogeneous mixtures or heterogeneous mixtures? Explain. (Go back and read about homogeneous and heterogeneous mixtures in Chapter 5).

 Make a list of all the devices that are used to separate mixtures.

 Can you design a new kind of "separating machine" that might be useful in separating a mixture. Draw a picture of your "machine" and write a description of how to make it. Write directions for using it.

 Examine a piece of granite. How many different components can you see? Write a description of each. Examine the granite using a binocular microscope. What can you see with the microscope that you missed with your naked eye? Write a description of what you see with the microscope.

For Parents and Teachers

Getting Started

Children always enjoy taking things apart. They also enjoy identifying and comparing objects. These processes are easily combined into activities which exemplify the process of separating mixtures. In the beginning it is best to separate mixtures of relatively large objects. The identification, classification, and sorting will then be based on concrete, easily sensed properties such as color, shape, weight, and hardness, rather than on the properties of invisible abstract bits (molecules). At appropriate points, refer children back to Chapter 5 on mixtures.

A beginning activity that children will enjoy is separating the components of commercially available trail mix, the snack hikers often use. Most children are familiar with it. Give each group of three children a cup of mix. They can sort the nuts, raisins, candies, and pieces of fruit (the actual composition will depend on the brand) into separate piles on clean pieces of paper.

Have children write descriptions of each component. They should indicate shape, size, color, and weight differences. They should also try and estimate the amount of each component by weight or volume. If you have a scale or balance this could be a quantitative comparison, but it doesn't need to be.

After the separation is complete, point out that the mixture has been separated into a certain number of different individual components (three, four, or more), and that each has *different properties*. You could have several different brands available so that their composition can be compared. Children can read the labels on the packages to see if they correspond to the separated components. At the end of the experiment, children can eat the separated mixture, perhaps comparing the quality and taste of the components.

The concept of a mixture is not only associated with solids, so children should also separate a mixture of liquids. A mixture of vegetable oil and water is convenient. This mixture can be made in a Mason jar. With the lid on, shake it vigorously. Have students observe that the oil slowly separates from the water and forms a layer on the top. Ask them how the mixture might be separated. They will probably suggest that the oil be poured off. You should have some clear plastic cups for them to pour it into. It might get a bit messy so be prepared with paper towels. Note that mixtures of liquids which don't form separate layers, but which dissolve in each other, are often much harder to separate (i.e., syrup and water or soda and milk). These are discussed below in *A Deeper Look*.

Another interesting experiment is the separation of a gas from a liquid. Soda is such a mixture, and the gas can be separated and collected simply by stretching the open end of a balloon over the top of a freshly opened bottle of soda. You should pour out a bit of the soda from the bottle before you do this so the balloon doesn't fill with foam. Once the balloon is in place the soda can be placed in warm or hot water and gently shaken.

The balloon will inflate as the gas leaves the liquid. It does so because the dissolved carbon dioxide gas is much less soluble in the hot than in the cold liquid, and also because the pressure is reduced with the cap off the soda bottle. When the cap is on, the high pressure in the bottle keeps the gas in the liquid. Children might taste the soda after the gas is gone to compare the quality and taste to freshly opened soda. The size of the inflated balloon provides a measure of the amount of gas in the soda. You could try different amounts of soda to see that smaller amounts have less dissolved gas.

A Deeper Look

There are many different ways of separating mixtures. The more components a mixture has, the more difficult it is to separate them. The methods used vary depending on whether the mixture is of several solids, or several liquids, or a solid in a liquid.

The easiest mixture to separate is one in which the component parts are solid, large, and visible. This is a heterogeneous mixture, which was discussed in Chapter 5. Heterogeneous mixtures of solids, of liquids and of solids in liquids can be separated by hand if the parts are sufficiently large. The separation of trail mix, described above, is such a case. If the solids in a heterogeneous mixture are small particles that cannot be separated by hand, other methods must be used. An example would be a mixture of sand, salt, and iron filings. This grayish mixture cannot be separated by hand. Separation of the components relies on the different properties of each component of the mixture.

Sand and iron filings are not soluble in water, but salt is. Iron filings are attracted to a magnet, but sand is not. This mixture can be separated by first adding water so the salt will dissolve. The salt water-sand-iron mixture can be poured through a coffee filter and the salt water will come through, leaving the sand and iron filings in the filter. *Filtration* is a useful way of separating a solid from a liquid (see diagram below).

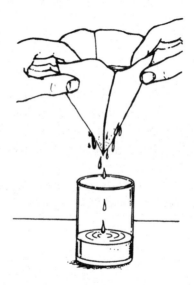

The salt water that comes through the filter is a homogeneous mixture of a solid (salt) dissolved in a liquid (water). The water in this mixture can be evaporated off and the salt can be recovered. The sand and iron filings can be dried, and a magnet can be run through the mixture to pull out all the iron. This is best done by putting the mixture on the top of a heavy piece of paper and dragging the magnet underneath over and over again. You avoid getting small particles of iron on the magnet. They are difficult to remove.

A heterogeneous mixture of two liquids (i.e., oil and water) can be separated by pouring off the one floating on top. It is difficult to get a clean separation this way, however. A

**Sand and iron filings mixture on a paper
being separated with a magnet**

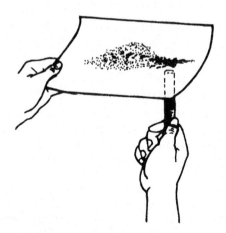

glass dropper with a rubber bulb can also be used to separate oil and water, though this takes much longer. Laboratories have glass *separatory funnels* which allow the lower layer to be drained off (see diagram below).

**Using a separatory funnel to separate
a heavy liquid from a lighter one**

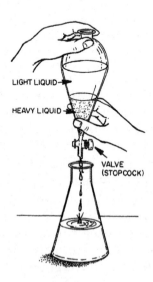

LIGHT LIQUID

HEAVY LIQUID

VALVE
(STOPCOCK)

In homogeneous mixtures the components are not separately visible, but are mixed together in such a way that the mixture looks like a single thing. An example of this is the salt water noted above, where salt is completely dissolved in water. Such mixtures are easily separated if the liquid is volatile and evaporates easily, as in the case of salt dissolved in water. Evaporation of the water leaves the salt behind, but the water part of the mixture is lost in this separation. It can be recovered if the mixture is heated and the water vapor which comes off is condensed. This is very similar to another type of separation called *distillation*.

In a distillation, a homogeneous mixture of two or more liquids is brought to a boil in a distillation flask. The liquid with the lower boiling point vaporizes first and passes through a condenser where it is cooled and converted back to a liquid and collected. The liquid with the next lowest boiling point vaporizes and is collected in the same fashion. In practice, this technique is not necessarily as simple as described here, but with very complex distillation equipment it works very well (see diagram below).

A simple distillation apparatus

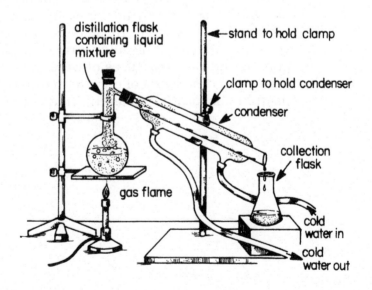

Another useful way of separating mixtures is to use *chromatography*. Chromatography is a technique that separates materials by allowing a solution or mixture of them to seep through an *adsorbent* (paper or other material) so that each compound separates out into a single layer or band. Often these bands are colored. A common example of this effect is when water is absorbed by a paper strip upon which a mixture of colored components has been placed. When the water seeps past the mixture, the components travel out of the spot along with the water, but at different rates. In this way, the colors which compose black ink are separated as described in the dialogue.

On a microscopic level, the molecules of each component are mixed together before the separation. As the water passes through the mixture, some molecules move more rapidly along with the water and some travel more slowly. The component molecules are thus separated out into groups. These appear as bands of color on the paper. Each band is a large collection of a single type of molecule.

The reason that components of the mixture travel at different rates is that each different type of molecule has a different attraction to the paper and to the water. Those most strongly attracted to the paper and least attracted to the water travel slower. Those less strongly attracted to the paper and most strongly attracted to the water travel more rapidly. The reason for these different attractions has to do with the different molecular structure of each colored component and the structures of water and the paper. There are many different kinds of chromatography which are very useful in separating different kinds of mixtures.

Getting In and Out of Shape

Freezing and Melting

> ❝ *Melting makes things soggy on the outside.* ❞

Bobby: Mommy, why do puddles make sheets of ice, like windows, in the morning?

Mother: Windows?

B: Yes, like sheets of glass, with water underneath them. They break when you step on them.

M: They're just sheets of ice. How do you make ice?

B: In the freezer.

M: The same thing happens outside when it's cold. The water changes to ice where it touches very cold air. When air is colder than the ground under the puddle, the top changes to ice but the bottom doesn't. And when the air warms up again, the top melts. You've seen that happen.

B: But what makes it do that? Why doesn't glass melt when it gets hot?

M: Is glass the same thing as ice?

B: Well, you can see through it like you can see through ice, but it isn't the same at all. It can't change to water.

M: Is ice the same thing as water?

B: No, it's not really the same either. It's more like glass because you can pick it up. You can't pick up water unless you put it in a glass. And water makes things wet. Ice doesn't.

M: But what happens when ice gets hot?

B: It changes to water. It melts.

M: And what does water do in the freezer?

B: It changes to ice. We just said that! It's called freezing.

M: So, it's one thing that has two forms. It's a solid when it's cold and it's a liquid when it's hot. When it changes from the solid to the liquid we call it melting, and when it changes from the liquid to the solid we call it freezing. It can go back and forth depending on how hot or cold it is.

B: You mean it's the same thing? Ice is solid water and regular water is—just water, or, melted ice?

M: That's right. One thing. Two forms. There are lots of things like that.

B: There are?

M: Sure. Think about breakfast this morning.

B: I had chocolate milk, pancakes, ham, and orange juice. None of those things changed into another form. Maybe when I ate them, and they went into my stomach then they. . . .

M: What about the pat of butter on your pancakes?

B: What about it?

M: What happened to it after I put it on your pancakes?

B: I ate it. With the pancakes and syrup.

M: I know you ate it. What happened to it before you ate it?

B: It melted all over the pancakes.

M: Where did the butter come from and what made it melt?

B: It came from the refrigerator. I guess the hot pancakes made it melt.

M: So the butter changed its form. From a solid pat to a liquid running all over your pancakes. You could pick up the solid pat but it would be very hard to pick up the melted butter, wouldn't it?

B: Like ice and water.

M: Yes, that's what I mean. Two forms, solid and liquid. Some things that are solid when they are cold change to liquids when they get hot. The forms change, but the things are really the same stuff.

B: But how does it happen? Why do things change from a solid form to a liquid form when they get hot? Cars and trucks don't melt when they get hot. And glass doesn't change. And. . . .

M: Well that's not really true. If it's hot enough those things also change. It's called melting, just like ice and butter melt. Metals and glass can melt too, but it's got to be very, very hot.

B: But trees don't melt when they get hot. When we build a fire in the fireplace, the logs don't melt. They just burn up into smoke. And ham doesn't melt in the pan, it just cooks, or burns up if you leave it in the pan too long.

M: That's true. Some things change into completely new things when they get hot. That's different than melting. When things melt, they don't become new things. They just change their form. And they can always go back the other way. Ice can melt to become water. And the water can freeze and become ice. All you have to do is make it hot or cold to make the water change.

B: What about the logs and the ham?

M: Burning logs change to something new which isn't wood anymore. Ashes, smoke, and water vapor. New things.

B: It's not melting is it?

M: No, it's not. You can't change the vapor, smoke, and ashes of a burned log back into a log again very easily can you? You can't freeze ashes and smoke and get a log.

132

B: How do you know what things will melt when they get hot and what things will change into new stuff when they get hot?

M: That's a tough question. Most things that are living, or were alive, don't melt. When they get really hot, they change into new things. Wood for example, and plants, bugs, flowers, and ham. None of those things melt. If they get really hot, they change into something different. And you can't get them back by cooling the new things they make.

B: Oᴋ, but what about the things like ice and butter that do melt when they get hot? What does hot do to them?

M: I don't think you mean to say "What does hot do to them?" We have to make a distinction between the words "heat" and "hot".

B: I thought they meant the same thing.

M: Not really. A teaspoon of hot water and a pot of hot water might both be at the same temperature—be just as hot—but there is a lot more heat in the pot of water than in the teaspoon. It's better to ask what heat does to ice.

B: Oᴋ. So what is heat, and how does it make ice and butter melt?

M: First, we have to know what ice, butter, and other things are made of. Then we can see what heat is and how it changes things.

B: So what are ice and butter made of?

M: You know what water is made of. Remember we talked about where rain came from? Remember the tiny bits that make up water?

B: Yes, I remember.

M: Well, ice is also made of the same tiny bits. And so is water vapor in the air, which forms clouds.

B: If water and ice and water vapor are all made of the same tiny bits, how come they're different?

M: That's the perfect question. The answer to that question explains what heat is and why it changes ice to water.

B: *So tell me then!*

M: In ice, the bits are very close together and they don't move very much. In water, they are a little farther apart and they are moving a bit more. In water vapor, they are very far apart and moving very fast.

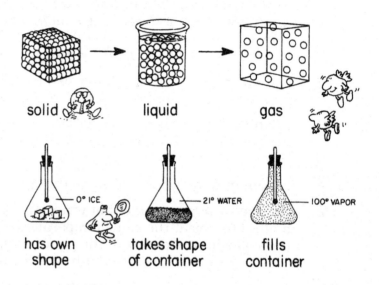

solid   liquid   gas

    0° ICE   21° WATER   100° VAPOR

has own shape   takes shape of container   fills container

B: I see. Ice holds its own shape because the bits are all stacked together, like in the crystal of sugar that Jose told me about. Liquid water is the same shape as the glass or bowl that it's in because the bits move around. They don't have a shape of their own. And water vapor goes all over into the air. The bits are so far apart we can't see them.

M: Yes. You've got the idea.

B: But what's heat and why does it change the ice to water?

M: Heat is just the *motion* of the bits. For a certain number of bits, *the more they move, the more heat there is.* So when you add heat to ice you make the bits start to move, and the crystal of ice starts to break down. It changes to water. They're the same bits as in the ice but they're moving around a lot more.

B: But where does the heat come from? *What is it?*

M: It's just the amount of movement of the bits of things. When they move fast there is more heat than when they move slowly. When you put an ice cube in a hot pan, the bits of the pan are moving back and forth very fast and cause the bits in the ice to start moving back and forth very fast as well. And then the ice changes into water. We can call this back-and-forth motion *vibrating.*

B: Why doesn't the pan change into water if its bits are vibrating so fast?

M: You mean why doesn't it change into a liquid.

B: Yes, that's what I mean. Why doesn't the pan melt like the ice?

M: Because the pan bits are much heavier and bigger than the ice bits. And metal bits stick to each other much tighter than the water bits. They have to vibrate very fast before the pan will change into a liquid. But it will do that if you add enough heat to it. You can melt the pan and get liquid metal. That's how they make cast iron pans. They melt the metal and pour it into a mold where it cools and gets solid.

B: It must be very hot.

M: Indeed it is. Much hotter than you need to melt ice!

B: So let's go back to what is "hot." And how is it different than "heat." When you talked about the pot of hot water and the teaspoon of hot water I got confused. And I'm still confused.

M: Think about two bathtubs filled with the same amount of water. In a hot bath the water bits are moving much faster than in a cold bath. So hot and cold are really just words meaning the relative amount of motion of the bits. There's more heat in the hot bathtub than the cold one. Heat is the total motion of the bits. But how much heat you have depends on how many bits there are. For instance, there's a lot more heat in a bathtub full of hot water than in a glass of hot water *at the same temperature.*

B: There is?

M: Yes, because there are fewer bits moving in the glass of water than in the tub, even though they're moving at the same average speed.

B: That's confusing.

M: A little. But if you think about it for a while, and maybe draw a few pictures of how the bits move and how many there might be in a glass of water or a bathtub full of hot water, it'll begin to make more sense.

B: What about freezing? How does water freeze?

M: The water bits just slow down when they are near cold things. Heat, the motion of the water bits, is transferred to the other things. And then the bits of the other things start moving faster. If that keeps on happening, the water bits slow down so much that they can line up close to each other and the water turns to a solid.

B: Ice?

M: Yes, ice. And if the ice gets near hot things it will melt as its bits come apart from the nice stack and start to move again.

B: If I get too hot will I melt? I've heard people say: "I'm so hot I'm melting."

M: They say that just to express how hot they feel. People don't really melt. But they can get burned. Remember the time you touched the burner on the stove?

B: Oh yes. It hurt a lot and made a blister on my finger. That's not like melting, is it Mommy?

M: No, it's more like a log burning.

B: I know something else that melts. Ice cream! Can I have a bowl?

M: What about dinner?

B: I want to watch the ice cream melt.

M: An experiment you mean. You're not going to eat it?

B: Well . . . I don't want to waste it after it melts do I?

M: It's nice you're concerned about waste, but what about your carrots at dinner last night?

B: But they weren't an experiment. They were just part of dinner.

M: Which you didn't like?

B: Which do you think melts faster, chocolate ice cream or vanilla ice cream?

M: I suppose you'll need a bowl of each to find out, right? For scientific purposes.

B: Yes!

M: I thought so.

Freezing and Melting–A Description

In Chapters 1 through 4 you learned that a pure substance can exist in three different forms, solid, liquid, and gas. For example, water can be solid ice, liquid water, or gaseous vapor. When it's very cold, water is a solid. When it's at normal temperatures, water is a liquid. When it's very hot, water is a vapor or gas. A metal like iron can also be a solid, liquid, or gas, but it must be very hot indeed for it to be a liquid, and even hotter for it to be gaseous. We will describe here the process of changing from a solid to a liquid, called melting. We'll also describe the reverse of this process, a liquid changing to a solid, called freezing.

You learned that a solid holds its own shape, a liquid takes the shape of its container, and a gas fills the container which holds it. We have said that solids, liquids, and gases are composed of very small bits, and the appearance of a substance (i.e., whether it's a solid, liquid or gas) depends on the arrangement and movements of these very small bits. In a solid, we can think of the bits as holding on to each other very tightly, not moving much at all. In a liquid, we can think of them as holding hands loosely, and changing hands with each other quite often as they move around from place to place. In a gas, we can think of them as not holding hands or touching at all, except when they crash into each other while zooming around.

Let's begin with the small bits of a substance not moving very much. If they are stacked in neat rows on top of each other, hugging very tightly, then the substance is in its solid form. A crystal is an example of a pure substance in its solid form. Ice is the solid crystalline form of water. In a solid, the bits are not moving about from place to place. The structure of a solid is rigid. It has a shape which doesn't change. You can pick it up and move it about. It still looks the same. The small bits remain in their positions in the solid.

SOLID

LIQUID

If you heat a solid like ice by letting it come into contact with something whose small bits are moving more rapidly (warm air for example) they will collide with the bits in the ice, causing them to begin to move slightly. If you keep the ice in the warm air, the ice bits will begin to shake a bit. Eventually they will begin to fall out of the solid array on the surface of the crystal. As more and more of them do this the ice crystal falls apart and changes. The bits move more freely about and we see liquid water forming as the solid crystal changes. This is the process of *melting*. The crystal of solid ice melts to liquid water. Adding heat to ice (making its bits move more rapidly) causes it to melt.

Liquid water looks different than solid ice. It moves about and takes the shape of whatever is holding it. If it is on a table, it spreads out into a thin film. If it's in a glass, it takes the shape of the inside of the glass. If we drink it, it takes the shape of the inside of our mouth and then our throat as it slides down into our stomach. The bits in the liquid easily move about from place to place. This is what makes a liquid fluid. If you look up *fluid* in the dictionary it will say: "flowing, changing, and moving." That does describe what a liquid is like, doesn't it?

Many solids can change into liquids, but the amount of heat needed to make them change is different from solid to solid. You probably have seen pictures of volcanos with melted rock flowing from them so you know rocks can melt. But the temperature at which they do this is very high and the heat needed is much more than the heat needed to melt ice. The small bits of rock hold on to each other much more tightly than the small bits of water.

The temperature where things melt is called their *melting point.* Different substances have different melting points. The melting point of ice is zero degrees centigrade or thirty-two degrees Fahrenheit. This temperature is very common in the winter, but not very common in the summer (if we are not near the north or south poles). In the summer it is usually much warmer, which is why ice does not form outside in the summer.

Many solids are not really pure things. Living things are an example. Flowers, trees, bugs, animals, fish, and people are really very complex mixtures of solids, liquids, and gases. Brick buildings, sidewalks, cars, clothing, and many other things around you, including this book, are mixtures of different solids. Sometimes when mixtures are heated they change into new things. This can occur when the components in the mixture combine with each other. Sometimes it happens when they combine with oxygen in the air. Even pure things sometimes break apart when they are heated. They decompose. These combinations and decompositions are called *reactions* and are the subject of Chapter 9. They are different than melting. An example of a reaction is the burning of a log. When a log is heated in air it doesn't melt. It changes to new solids and gases (ashes, water, vapor, and carbon dioxide).

When a liquid like water cools, the bits that are moving around slow down. They don't travel as far as when the liquid is hot. If the liquid gets colder and colder, eventually the bits will slow down so much that they will begin to collect together in clumps. These little clumps are like tiny crystals. Once they form, more and more liquid bits collect on their surface as the liquid cools. Eventually enough will collect together so that a small crystal of solid can be seen. In liquid water which is cooling like this, small ice crystals will form. As the water continues to cool, the ice crystals will get bigger and bigger as more water bits collect on their surface. Water which is doing this is *freezing*. Freezing is the opposite of melting. Any liquid can freeze just like this. The process of freezing is simply the slowing down of fast moving bits in the liquid until they eventually come together into a solid array.

When liquid rock (lava) squirts up out of a volcano and hits the relatively cool air, this is exactly what happens. The liquid cools and forms a solid.

Melting

a piece of ice   ice on heated pan   ice on heated pan   melted ice on heated pan

Experiments

YOU WILL NEED:

plastic place mat	frying pan
1 white & 1 dark-	ice cubes
colored place	butter
mat	salt
plate	rubbing alcohol
thermometer	vegetable oil
glasses	honey
soldering iron	metal solder
	piece of wood

 Take two ice cubes out of the freezer. Put one on a plastic place mat in the sun. Put the other on an *identical* plastic place mat in the shade. Observe each cube and make a record of your observations (both words and pictures). What happens? What causes the behavior of the two cubes to be different?

 Try the same experiment using a white place mat and a darkly colored place mat. Do you notice any difference?

 Take a cube of butter on a plate and put it in the shade. Watch what happens. Do the same thing with another butter cube in the hot sun. What differences do you notice after a while?

141

Put five ice cubes in a glass and then fill it half full with water. Put a thermometer in the glass and measure the temperature every half hour. (This thermometer must be able to go down to the freezing point of water.) Make sure you mix the ice and water well before you read each temperature.

 Continue to write down the temperature and time every half hour or so until about an hour after all the ice has melted. Each time you do this write a brief description of the glass of cubes and water. Plot a graph of temperature versus time, noting at each time how much ice is left (get help from your parents or teacher with the graph if you don't know how to make one). Be patient. This experiment takes quite a while and you don't have to sit and watch it all the time. What happens to the temperature as the ice is melting? What happens to the temperature of the water after all the ice has melted.

 On another day do the same experiment, but this time add ten large tablespoons of salt to the glass of ice and water. What do you notice about the temperature this time?

 Place a glass of rubbing alcohol and a glass of water in the freezer part of your refrigerator (get your parent's permission). Leave them there for five or six hours before you check them. What do you see? What can you say about the temperature at which water freezes compared to the temperature at which rubbing alcohol freezes?

 Try this same experiment with a glass of water and a glass of vegetable oil. What do you notice? Vegetable oil is not a pure substance. It is a mixture, and this affects how it behaves when it is cooled. Can you describe in detail the properties of the cold oil compared to oil at room temperature? Could this difference be due to the behavior of the small bits that make up the oil?

 Try the same experiment with a glass of honey. Honey is not a pure substance either.

 With your parent's help, touch a piece of metal solder with a hot soldering iron. What do you see? Is there anything similar to your observations about melting and freezing water? Does solder melt in the hot sun? Why or why not? How come liquid solder turns solid so quickly when you take the soldering iron away?

 With your parent's help, touch a small piece of wood with a hot soldering iron. What do you see? How is this different from touching a piece of solder? Is the wood melting? If not, why not? What is happening?

 With your parent's help, put an ice cube in a hot frying pan. What do you see? What do you think is happening to the small bits which make up the ice where it touches the bottom of the hot frying pan? Can you see ice changing to liquid water? Can you see liquid water changing to water vapor? Why doesn't the hot frying pan melt like the ice?

Questions to Write and Draw

 Draw a picture and write a description of how ice melts to liquid water. In your picture show the small water bits in an ice cube and how they are arranged. Show what happens to the arrangement and the motion of the bits in the ice as it melts into liquid water. Show the motion and arrangement of bits in the liquid water which forms.

 What do you think heat is? Make a list of hot things you know and cold things you know. What happens when a hot thing touches a cold thing? Give some examples and write a description. Draw a picture of what happens, showing the motion of small bits in the hot thing and the cold thing.

 What do you think temperature is? How can you find the temperature of something? Is it easier to find the temperature of water than the temperature of a stone? Put a thermometer in the refrigerator and another thermometer in the freezer part of the refrigerator. Check later and see if these parts of the refrigerator are at different temperatures. Write the temperatures down. Put a glass of water in the refrigerator and another glass of water in the freezer part of the refrigerator. Check them every half hour and write a description of what you see. Do you know where the name "freezer" comes from?

 Write a list of all the things that you have seen melt. Write a list of all the things that you have seen freeze. What causes things to melt? What causes things to freeze?

 If the liquid in a thermometer shrinks a bit when it gets colder and expands a bit when it gets hotter, can you explain how a thermometer might work?

What causes butter to melt when you put it on hot pancakes or in a hot frying pan? Could you explain this by the movement of the small bits that make up butter?

 Why does it snow in the winter but not in the summer? What makes snow melt on a warm day?

For Parents and Teachers

Getting Started

Children who live in climates where the temperature in winter routinely goes well below zero degrees centigrade (the temperature at which water freezes or ice melts) know well the various solid forms that water can take. They have experienced them directly in the air and on the ground under their feet (ice, hail, sleet, slush, and the various forms of snow). All children are familiar with the processes of melting and freezing water, either from nature, or because of their experience with ice cubes from the freezer portion of the refrigerator. Even so, many of them may not completely understand the process, especially as it applies to other kinds of materials. Very few children have seen melted rock, steel, or glass. So it is best to begin with things children have seen melt, like water, butter, ice cream, and ice pops, and extend the concept from there.

You can do the following experiments and dialogue at home with a child, or they can be done in a classroom setting. In a classroom, have children do it in groups of three. If you prefer you can demonstrate it to the whole group. If the latter, begin the discussion by having children sit in a semicircle with a warm hot plate in the center. Place a small, clear Pyrex® bowl or casserole containing five or six large ice cubes on the hot plate. Make sure that the hot plate is not too hot, for if it is, the glass might crack. This is especially so if you put the container on the hot plate empty, let it get too hot, and then add ice. It is best to have the cubes already in it before you place the container on the hot plate, which should only be very warm to the touch.

Ask the children to observe and describe what happens when the container of ice is placed on the hot plate. This can be done in a journal if they are working in small groups, or you can write their comments down on a transparency, the blackboard, or a piece of paper. Choose which is most appropriate for the size of your group. You might get comments such as: "the ice is melting, the ice is changing to water, the ice cubes are getting smaller, the ice is dissolving, the ice cubes are moving, water is coming or appearing, or getting bigger, etc."

If the process of dissolving is mentioned you should make a distinction between that (see Chapter 3) and what they are seeing when ice melts. Important comments to focus on are the *increasing amount of water and the diminishing size of the cubes.* You might take them out of the container so they can see this decrease in size more directly.

If you want, you could pour off the water into another container briefly, noting the amount, and then quickly pour it back onto the remaining ice. This could be done over fixed intervals of time, and a graph of the height of water in the container versus time could be made.

You might also wish to have a thermometer in the ice-water mixture. If you do, you should note to the children that the temperature will stay at zero degrees centigrade (thirty-two degrees Fahrenheit) until all the ice is melted. After that the temperature of the water will slowly increase. Make sure you stir the ice-water mixture well each time before you read the temperature.

Ask children to list the properties of ice and water. Focus their attention on the differences among these properties. The most concrete is that ice can be picked up with your fingers, whereas to pick up water you have to make a container with your hands. The discussion should proceed to how descriptions of solids and liquids serve to define them. You can't push your fingers through a solid, but you can with a liquid. The fact that ice has its own shape whereas water takes the shape of its container should evolve. This then leads to the conclusion that water can have two forms, solid (ice) and liquid. Ask them how to make ice change to water, and how to make water change to ice. This should lead to the concept of heating or cooling, that heating ice changes it to water whereas cooling water can change it back to ice. Emphasize the reversible nature of the process.

Focus the discussion towards the microscopic nature of substance, and how the motion of small bits can be related to the processes of melting and freezing. You can place a petri dish of BBs on the overhead projector. The image on the screen represents the tiny bits of solid in an unmoving array. (The BBs should be stacked one against another. This can be achieved by slightly tilting the dish if the projector surface is not already slightly tilted.) The outline of the top row of BBs represents the surface of the "solid" shape. By gently shaking the dish, the BBs will move about and roll towards the bottom of the tilted dish, representing a liquid. Make sure you tilt the dish in the right direction so that the "bottom" of the container is on the bottom of the screen and not the top.

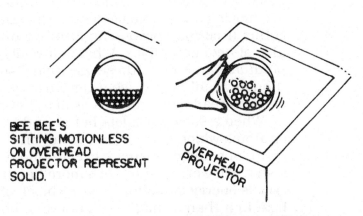

BEE BEE'S SITTING MOTIONLESS ON OVERHEAD PROJECTOR REPRESENT SOLID.

OVERHEAD PROJECTOR

BEE BEE'S IN SLANTED PETRI DISH ON OVERHEAD PROJECTOR. SLIGHT MOTION REPRESENTS LIQUID.

If you wish, you may purchase a molecular motion demonstrator which sits on the overhead projector and achieves these effects (including vaporization to a gas) automatically. The machine is expensive ($288.90), but does a good job of allowing children to visualize solids, liquids, and gases in terms of the movement and arrangement of small bits [Molecular Motion Demonstrator: Carolina Biological Supply Co., 2700 York Road, Burlington, NC 27215].

Relate the models of an unmoving array of bits (solid) and a loose moving collection of bits (liquid) to the properties of solid ice and liquid water. Point out the unchanging shape or outline of the unmoving array of BBs and compare it to the fluid moving BBs with a relatively flat surface, like the surface of a liquid. The motion of the BBs can be related to the temperature. The more rapid the motion, the higher the temperature. The number of BBs can be related to the total heat content of the sample. The more BBs there are moving at a particular speed, the more heat.

A Deeper Look

The processes of melting and freezing are essentially the same. The only difference between them is the direction of heat flow—whether the molecules or atoms of the substance are moving away from each other (melting) or coming together (freezing). Beyond an intuitive understanding, the idea of *heat* is complex. What is it really, and what is *temperature?* Answering these questions isn't too easy, even though we all "know" what they are: Heat makes ice melt and you read temperatures from a thermometer.

When a substance gets hotter and hotter, the molecules or atoms which compose it ("small bits" in the children's descriptions and dialogue) move around or vibrate much faster. They are said to have more kinetic energy. Kinetic energy is energy of motion. A large block of iron will have more heat in it than a small block of iron if both blocks are at the same temperature. Similarly, a large glass of water at twenty-five degrees centigrade will have more heat in it than a small glass of water at the same temperature. *The amount of heat contained in a substance depends on how much substance you have, and how fast the atoms or molecules in the substance are vibrating or moving.*

In both small and large glasses of water, at twenty-five degrees centigrade, water molecules move at the same average rate. That is another way of saying that the water in both samples is at the same temperature. But there are

148

more water molecules in the large glass of water and therefore it contains more heat. Temperature is just a measure of the average motion (speed) of the molecules in the substance whereas heat is a measure of the total motion of the molecules in the substance. It is easy to measure the temperature of a substance with a thermometer. To measure the heat content of a substance, you also need to know how much you have (the mass of the substance).

If two objects at different temperatures are placed in contact with each other, an interesting thing happens. The hot one will cool down and the cold one will warm up until they are both the same temperature. *Heat (molecular motion) always flows from the hot object to the cold one. We can define temperature this way.* If heat flows from one thing to another then they are at different temperatures. If it doesn't flow, they are at the same temperature. As something cools its molecules lose kinetic energy (they slow down). As something is heated, its molecules gain kinetic energy (they speed up).

Temperature is an *intensive* property of a substance. It doesn't depend on how much you have, but only on how fast the molecules in the substance are moving. Heat is an *extensive* property of a substance. How much you have depends on how much substance you have. The more substance at a particular temperature, the more heat there is. Cooking an egg to where it is hard-boiled shows this easily (once the egg is hard-boiled, you can stop cooking it). If you heat three gallons of water to boiling (about one-hundred degrees centigrade), turn off the heat source, and add an egg, it will harden completely. If you do the same thing with a cup of water at one hundred degrees centigrade, the egg will not cook completely. There is not enough heat available in the cup of hot water to cook the egg, but there is plenty in the three gallons.

Now let's apply these ideas of heat and temperature to the melting of ice to give water, and the freezing of water to give ice. These are called *changes of state*, i.e., from a solid to a liquid, or from a liquid to a solid. They involve heat transfer—a change in the amount of molecular motion of the water molecules.

If you take a piece of ice out of the freezer at ten degrees below zero centigrade and let it sit on a table at room temperature it will not melt immediately. It is in contact with both the table and the air in the room, and heat from these (molecular motion of the air and table molecules) will be transferred to the water molecules in the ice. The air around the ice and the table beneath it will begin to cool (their molecules will move and vibrate less rapidly) and the ice will begin to warm up (water molecules in the ice will vibrate more rapidly).

The temperature of the ice will increase until it reaches zero degrees centigrade. There is not enough ice to cool the table and air down, so heat keeps on flowing into the ice. However, *the temperature of the ice does not increase beyond zero degrees centigrade.* Instead, the heat flowing into it causes the vibrating molecules of water in the crystal lattice, which have been vibrating more and more rapidly as heat flows in, to break free from each other. There is a weak attraction between water molecules in the crystal lattice of ice. This attraction holds the molecules together in the lattice. As heat flows into the ice—as the water molecules begin to move and vibrate slightly—this weak intermolecular attraction is overcome and the individual water molecules break away from the crystal lattice. The ice begins to melt.

All the heat flowing into the ice at this point goes into melting the ice and *separating* the water molecules from each other, not to increasing the temperature. *The temperature of the ice-water mixture will remain at zero degrees centigrade, even as more heat from the air and table flow into it, until all the ice is melted.*

Once the ice has completely changed to a liquid, heat flowing in from the table and air will start to increase the temperature of the melted water. The water temperature (a measure of the speed of the moving water molecules) will now increase until it becomes the same as that of the air and the table.

All the concepts described for the melting and freezing of water apply to the melting and freezing of any solid or liquid. For most metallic or ionic, inorganic solids, like iron or salt, the temperatures and amounts of heat required for changes of state are much greater than for changes of state of water. Of course, many solids, particularly organic or once living materials, simply decompose or undergo other reactions when they are heated. These changes are not melting. They are *chemical changes* in which new substances are formed (see Chapter 9). Such reactions are often oxidations, reactions with the air in the atmosphere, commonly called burning. Some compounds simply decompose all by themselves, because the molecules that compose them are unstable. For example, table sugar if heated rapidly, will decompose. If heat is applied very slowly it will melt before it decomposes.

When molecules undergo a chemical change, the atoms which are bonded together come apart. They recombine in various ways to give new molecules. Melting is not a chemical change. The molecules remain the same. There are weak bonds between molecules in a solid which hold them together in the crystal lattice. When these weak bonds break, the solid crystal melts to a liquid, but the molecules remain intact. They just move around more rapidly. The substance is still the same. It just changes its state from a solid to a liquid. Freezing is just the reverse of the melting process. During freezing the molecules slow down enough so that weak attractive forces can bring them together into the crystal lattice, and the liquid changes to its solid form.

Making Bubbles

Boiling

> *Boiling is like hot sauce and fire.*

Maria: Daddy, why does water turn to soda when it gets hot?

Father: Soda? Water doesn't turn to soda when it gets hot.

M: Yes it does. It gets lots of little bubbles in it, and they rise up to the top just like the bubbles in soda do.

F: It's not the same though, is it? What's the difference between soda and hot water?

M: Soda is cold. Hot water is hot.

F: How come cold water doesn't have bubbles in it, but hot water does?

M: Heating the water makes the bubbles, I think.

F: Ok, but what about soda? What makes the bubbles in soda?

M: Soda comes with bubbles in it. They don't come up until you open the bottle though. So opening the bottle of cold soda makes soda bubbles and heating water makes water bubbles.

F: It's not really the same then, is it? Soda and water are different. What about bottles of plain water? If you open them bubbles don't form.

154

M: So soda must have the bubbles already in it, and when you open the bottle they come out.

F: That's so. Soda is a liquid that has a gas dissolved in it. It's a solution of a gas in a liquid.

M: I remember talking to Diana about solutions. They're mixtures, aren't they?

F: Yes, they are. Soda is a mixture of flavored liquid with a gas dissolved in it. And when you open the bottle the gas comes out.

M: Water from the faucet doesn't have that gas dissolved in it, does it?

F: No, it doesn't.

M: Then what makes the bubbles come up in hot water on the stove in a pot? The water in the pot came from the faucet.

F: You already know that. You said that heating water makes bubbles form and rise up.

M: But how can that happen if there is no gas dissolved in the water to come out? Are the bubbles in hot water a gas?

F: Yes they are, but they aren't the same gas as in soda.

M: So there is a gas dissolved in water?

F: Not the gas that's in soda. But the heat can change water itself to a gas.

M: The heat changes water to a gas? How can it do that?

F: What do you know about liquids and gases?

M: Diana told me about water evaporating to a gas. She told me it changes to water vapor. That's a gas, isn't it. I know that water is made up of tiny bits that move around, and the warmer it is the faster they move. When water evaporates, the bits jump into the air and form a gas, but the water doesn't have to be boiling for it to evaporate.

F: What else do you notice when bubbles form in hot water?

M: The bubbles rise up to the top and then they pop, just like soda bubbles. And then steam comes off.

F: Do you see steam from soda?

M: Of course not, Daddy. Soda isn't hot!

F: What is steam?

M: Water turning to water vapor, a gas?

F: The steam is a collection of very tiny droplets of water that are turning . . . changing to invisible water vapor, a gas. That's why the steam rapidly disappears. It turns into water vapor, which is invisible.

M: OK, but what about the bubbles? Why do they form? Why doesn't hot water just evaporate and change to a gas like a puddle does? There are no bubbles in a puddle that's evaporating. And puddles don't steam. They just sit there and slowly disappear into a gas even when the water isn't boiling! Why doesn't hot water just sit and disappear like that? And I want to know about the bubbles!!

F: Well, if you boil it long enough it will disappear won't it? Eventually?

M: Yes. But what about the bubbles? Why are they forming?

F: Think about the water bits that are moving around faster and faster as we heat the water.

M: OK. The ones at the top of the water can jump out and change to water vapor, just like when a puddle evaporates.

F: That's true, they can. But what about the ones in the middle of the pot of water, or at the bottom? What will they do if we keep heating the water hotter and hotter?

M: They'll move faster and faster won't they?

F: They will. And if we keep on heating the water?

M: They'll go even faster.

F: They'd probably be bumping into each other more and more if the water was getting hotter and hotter wouldn't they?

M: I guess they would.

F: And if they started banging into each other faster and harder they would push themselves apart from each other wouldn't they?

M: But where would they go? If they push themselves apart they would just bump into other bits that were also moving faster and bumping into them harder and harder.

F: That's true. They would have a hard time being next to each other like the bits are in a liquid. They'd keep pushing each other apart.

M: Well, the ones on the surface of the water can leave by jumping out into the air. But the ones in the middle are just stuck in there, aren't they? Water in the middle of the pot can't evaporate.

F: No, it can't evaporate, but it can change into a gas.

M: How can it do that?

F: If the water gets hot enough, it can do that throughout the whole pot. The temperature at which water does that is called the boiling point. At the boiling point, liquid water changes to a gas throughout the liquid. The boiling point of water is 100 degrees centigrade or 212 degrees Fahrenheit.

M: How does it do that?

F: The bits are moving so fast at the boiling point, they push so hard against each other, that they form a gas right in the middle of the water, or on the bottom of the pot where it's the hottest.

M: And the bits have to get farther apart to make a gas? Is that how the bubbles form?

F: Yes!

M: So the bubbles in the boiling water aren't like soda bubbles then?

F: No, they're filled with water vapor, which is very hot. Soda bubbles are from a gas that's dissolved in the liquid soda, and they're cold.

M: Why do water vapor bubbles in boiling water rise up like soda bubbles?

F: Because gases are always lighter than the liquids, so water vapor bubbles rise in boiling water, just like dissolved soda gas bubbles rise in soda when you take the cap off the bottle.

M: And when they get to the top they pop?

F: They do indeed. And they release their water vapor at the surface.

M: And if it keeps happening over and over, bubbles rising up and popping, again and again, the water will all disappear.

F: Eventually it will, yes. It's called boiling.

M: It would take a long time.

F: It does take some time, but usually not as much time as it takes a puddle to evaporate.

M: What about soda? If I leave a glass of soda on the table the bubbles keep rising to the top and popping, but the soda doesn't disappear.

F: Remember, the soda bubbles aren't water vapor. They're formed from the gas that's dissolved in the soda. It's different. When all the soda bubbles have risen and popped, the dissolved gas is all gone leaving the liquid soda behind.

M: That's when the soda doesn't taste so good any more.

F: That's right. When soda loses all its bubbles we say it has gone flat.

M: Flat? It doesn't look flat. It looks the same. It just doesn't have any more bubbles.

F: It's just a way of talking about it.

M: Could we dissolve that gas in plain water and make it bubble when it isn't hot?

F: But that's quite common. It's called seltzer or sparkling water. It doesn't have any flavors or sugar, and when it goes flat it tastes very much like plain water.

M: Seltzer or sparkling water?

F: Yes. Sometimes it's called carbonated water because the gas that's dissolved in it is called carbon dioxide.

M: Is that the same gas in orange soda and cherry soda and. . . .

F: The very same, yes. It's the same gas in all the soda we drink.

M: Daddy, what would happen if we boiled orange soda? Would the bubbles that come up be carbon dioxide or soda vapor?

F: You mean carbon dioxide or water vapor.

M: Do I?

F: Yes. Soda is mainly water with small amounts of colored dye, sugar, flavorings, and carbon dioxide gas dissolved in it. The dye, sugar, and flavorings are dissolved solids, so the only thing that bubbles out of soda is the dissolved gas, the carbon dioxide.

M: But if we boil the soda there could be two kinds of bubbles, the carbon dioxide bubbles and the water vapor bubbles. What would happen then?

F: The carbon dioxide would bubble off first because it's not very soluble in hot soda. And if we keep on heating the soda, eventually the water in the soda would start to form bubbles of water vapor.

M: And the soda would be boiling then.

F: Yes. It would.

M: And the bubbles wouldn't be like the bubbles that form when we open the bottle from the refrigerator?

F: No, they wouldn't.

M: I wonder what it would taste like?

F: Hot boiled soda?

M: Yes! I drink hot chocolate don't I? Why couldn't I try hot boiled orange soda?

159

F: Well, I guess you could. But I think it tastes better cold with lots of carbon dioxide bubbles in it.

M: Daddy, how do they dissolve the carbon dioxide gas in the soda?

F: Let's talk about that later.

M: We could make carbonated milk couldn't we? And carbonated ice cream? And what about carbonated tomato juice?

F: Enough for today, Maria.

Boiling—A Description

At normal room temperatures water is a liquid. When it's very hot, water can become a vapor or gas. We will describe here the process of water changing from a liquid to a gas at a high temperature, well above room temperature. This is called boiling or vaporization. It is the opposite of the process called condensing (Chapter 2). Vaporization is similar to evaporation except that it happens at a higher temperature. Evaporation occurs when water turns into a vapor at the surface of the liquid. Vaporization of boiling water occurs throughout the liquid, not just on the surface.

As you learned earlier, liquid water is a large collection of bits moving about from place to place throughout the liquid. As water is heated, the bits move faster and faster. We can think of them as letting go of each other's hands and running more rapidly about. As the temperature is increased they will begin to bump into each other with greater and greater force. If the temperature is high enough, the bits will collide together so hard that they bounce far away from each other. The spaces between them will increase and the liquid will eventually turn into a gas, water vapor. At this temperature vapor will form throughout the liquid. Spherical bubbles of water vapor form in the hot liquid water and rapidly rise to the surface because they are lighter than the liquid. At the surface they burst, releasing the vapor to the air.

Most liquids will change into gases when heated to a high enough temperature, but the amount of heat needed to do this is quite different from liquid to liquid. Liquids which boil at temperatures which are lower than the boiling point of water are often called volatile. Not only do they boil at lower temperatures, they evaporate more readily. Alcohol is an example of a liquid that boils at a lower temperature than water.

Some liquids boil at temperatures much higher than water. Whether liquids boil at higher or lower temperatures depends on how big their bits are and how tightly the bits stick together in the liquid. You could think of liquids with high boiling temperatures as holding hands much tighter than liquids with lower boiling temperatures. Larger bits often move more slowly than smaller bits, and so their boiling temperatures are often higher. Liquid iron boils at a much much higher temperature than liquid water. Solid iron also melts at a much higher temperature than ice. The bits of iron are much heavier than the bits of water, and iron bits hold on to each other much more tightly than water bits.

Boiling

| a container of water—cold | a container of water—warm | a container of water—hot | a container of water—boiling |

The temperature at which liquids boil is called their *boiling point.* Different liquids have different boiling points (boiling temperatures). The boiling point of liquid water is one-hundred degrees centigrade or two-hundred and twelve degrees Fahrenheit. This temperature is not normally reached on the surface of the earth except in volcanic areas. In those areas however, jets and geysers of water vapor and boiling pools of water are quite common.

Many liquids are not really pure substances. Soda, milk, juice, gasoline, and oil are examples of liquids which are really mixtures of two or more different liquids or solids dissolved in liquids (see Chapter 5). When these mixtures are heated, the lower boiling components will vaporize first. If solids are dissolved in a liquid, they will be left behind after the liquid is vaporized or evaporated. This is useful in separating the components of a mixture and the technique is briefly discussed in Chapter 6.

Experiments

YOU WILL NEED: microwave
pot   spaghetti
thermometer   soda
plate   ground sugar
Pyrex® glass pot   crystals
  or metal pot

All these experiments should be done with adult supervision!

 The next time your parents cook spaghetti, carefully make a note of how long it takes the water in the pot to boil. Does it stop boiling for a while after the spaghetti is added? Why? Does it start boiling again? Why does this happen?

POT OF BOILING WATER

POT OF BOILING WATER IMMEDIATELY AFTER SPAGHETTI IS ADDED

 With your parent's permission, with a thermometer used in making fudge, measure the temperature of a pot of water taken right out of the cold tap. **With a parent present,** heat the water on the stove, taking the temperature every two minutes. What is the temperature when the water is boiling? Does it continue to go up as water boils? Why or why not? Hold a plate over the vapor coming from the boiling water. What happens? (Review Chapter 2 on Condensing).

 Along with a parent, boil a pot of 7-Up® or some other clear soda in a Pyrex® glass pot (a metal pot will do if you don't have a glass pot at home). Pour the cold soda out of a freshly opened bottle from the refrigerator directly into the pot. Keep a record of your observations. Are the bubbles which come up in the beginning the same as those which come up from the boiling soda? How are they different? After you have boiled the soda for ten minutes, let it cool to room temperature. Is it still carbonated? Taste it. What has happened?

 Along with a parent, heat a cup of water to boiling in the microwave. Remove it and add a small sample of finely ground sugar crystals. Why does the liquid foam up? What is happening? This is an example of superheating. Sometimes very hot water needs a place for the liquid to form bubbles and change to a vapor. The finely ground sugar crystals provide spots where vapor bubbles can form.

 When a pot of boiling water is removed from the heat, how long does it take to stop boiling? Why? How long does it take a glass of soda to stop bubbling? Why?

Questions to Write and Draw

 Write a description of how water boils. Draw a picture of liquid water changing into water vapor that shows the small water bits in liquid water and how they are arranged. Show what happens to the arrangement and the motion of the bits as the liquid water changes to gaseous water.

 What do you think would happen if you boiled water in a container which was covered on top with a large balloon *(do not do this experiment)*?

DO NOT DO THIS EXPERIMENT!

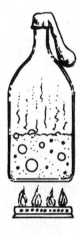

 Why might alcohol boil at a lower temperature than water? If you boiled a mixture of alcohol and water, which liquid would turn to vapor first? If the alcohol vapor left the mixture while it boiled, would the temperature of the boiling mixture change? Why or why not?

Why doesn't a puddle of water boil in the hot sun? How can it change to vapor (evaporate) without boiling?

 What is the difference between boiling and evaporation?

 Write a list of all the things you have seen boil. Are most of these composed mainly of water? Would oil boil if you heated it? **(Do not try this!)**

 Write a list of all the things you have seen evaporate.

 Why doesn't the temperature of boiling water get higher when you keep adding heat to it?

 How is boiling different than melting? How is it similar to melting? Use a diagram of the arrangement and movement of the tiny bits which compose water to explain.

 What is the opposite of boiling?

For Parents and Teachers

Getting Started

The concept of boiling must be approached with great care. Boiling water is dangerous and can cause severe burns. Nevertheless, because concepts of melting, freezing, boiling, and condensing are closely related processes, it is important to include boiling in your discussions of physical change. All children have seen pots of water boiling in the kitchen during food preparation and most are aware of the danger. You should emphasize this again before you begin this section so that children are reminded of it.

Review the concept of mixtures in Chapter 5. Begin by having children examine an unopened bottle of clear soda (7-Up®, Sprite®, or seltzer). Have them write a description of the liquid in order to compare it with the liquid after the cap is removed. Clear soda in a colorless container helps make viewing easier. You may wish to pour it into a glass. Have the children describe what happens when the cap is removed by writing and/or drawing pictures and diagrams. Have them volunteer their descriptions and collect these on a transparency, the blackboard, or a piece of paper.

Your list likely will contain items like: bubbles, fizzes, gas forms, foaming, hissing, etc. You might pour out some cups of soda for them to drink so they can experience the gaseous evolution by touch and taste, as well as by sight and sound. Note that soda is a mixture of a gas dissolved in a liquid.

Fill a clear glass Pyrex® flat-bottomed bowl or casserole with water and place it on a hot plate in front of the children. A small piece of broken porcelain or other porous material in the container will help insure smooth boiling. Turn the hot plate heat on high and have children keep a record of what they see and hear during the next ten minutes. You can prompt them if they don't make progress. You might tell them to draw what they see. They might observe and write down the following: sound of water boiling, bubble formation, steam formation, water motion, variation in water clarity as density changes, etc. Have them share descriptions with each other. While sharing, they may revise and add to them if they wish. Have them list differences between bubbling soda water and bubbling boiling water.

Begin a discussion of water as a collection of small bits moving faster and faster as the water is heated. Draw a picture of bubble formation in terms of rapidly moving small bits (see the picture in the Description of Boiling). Show how these rise to the surface and burst open, discharging vapor into the air. If you have access to the molecular motion machine noted in Chapter 7, place it on the overhead projector and "raise the temperature" by increasing the motion until the ball bearings "change from a liquid to a vapor." Alternatively, you could use a small petri dish of BBs as was done in Chapter 7 to illustrate melting. To illustrate vaporization simply shake the dish more rapidly.

A Deeper Look

Review Chapter 7 on melting and freezing, as well as the concepts of heat and temperature discussed there. The process of boiling is simply a continuation of the sequence of heating a solid, melting it, and heating the resultant liquid. If heating is continued, vaporization of the liquid to the gaseous state will occur. The changes that occur as the solid changes to a liquid and then to a gas are of two types: 1) heat makes the atoms or molecules of any phase move more rapidly and thus increases the temperature, and 2) as higher temperatures are reached, the material can change from one phase to another. In the discussion to follow, water is used as an example since these processes are commonly observed for ice, liquid water, and water vapor. However, they can occur for any liquid. In the diagram, changes of type 1) are represented by the horizontal line portion of the graph where the temperature is constant and water is changing from one phase to another (ice to water or water to steam). Changes of type 2) are represented by the curved portions of the line where a single phase (solid, liquid, or gas) is increasing in temperature.

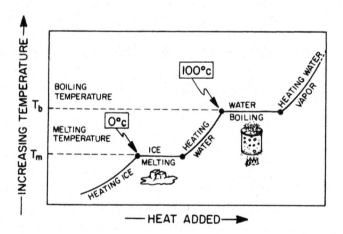

Heating ice makes the molecules (bits) vibrate more rapidly. When the *melting point* is reached the solid ice crystal changes to liquid water. The temperature of the ice-water mixture remains at zero degrees centigrade, even while heat is added, until all the ice is melted. If heating continues, the water will increase in temperature until it reaches one-hundred degrees centigrade. This is the *boiling point* of water. Water molecules are now moving fast enough to change into vapor, and bubbles will form throughout the liquid. The molecules contain sufficient energy of motion in the hot liquid so that the change to vapor occurs readily. The temperature of the water-vapor mixture will remain at one-hundred degrees centigrade, even while heat is added, until all of the liquid water has changed into vapor. If the vapor could be trapped and heated, its temperature would continue to rise and its volume would expand. This whole sequence is illustrated in the graph of temperature vs. heat added shown above. The curved portions of the graph represent the heating of a single phase (solid, liquid, or gas). The flat portions of the graph represent the change from one phase to another at constant temperature.

Boiling is a phase change, just like melting is a phase change. In each case water changes its state. During vaporization, all the heat energy supplied to the boiling liquid water goes into separating the molecules from each other. The result is a change from a large *visible collection* of molecules packed loosely together (the liquid) to a large *invisible collection* of molecules with large spaces between them (the vapor). The vapor takes up much more space than the liquid. A large tablespoon of liquid water would occupy a very large balloon if vaporized.

The term "boiling" is a lay term. A more technical term is vaporizing, which has an even broader meaning. Substances such as "dry ice" (solid carbon dioxide) can change from the solid to the gaseous state directly. This is also called vaporization. A more specific name for the process by which a solid changes directly to a gas is *sublimation*. You have all seen dry ice before. It does not melt. Over a period of time it just *sublimes* into a gas. Other solids which do this are moth balls and iodine crystals. The iodine you buy in the drugstore is really a solution of iodine crystals in alcohol (called tincture of iodine). Pure iodine is a purple crystalline solid. If it is left out in the open air it simply changes to a gas and floats away. Since iodine is very toxic, care must be taken when handling the solid.

Making Something New

Reacting

> *Reacting happens when someone pulls your hair and it hurts.*

Diana: Where does the wood in the fireplace go when it burns up? There's only a small pile of ashes left and the logs are all gone! Where did they go?

Mother: Is that all that happens when wood burns? Do you see anything else?

D: In the beginning there was lots of smoke, too. But once the fire got real hot there wasn't much smoke either. The wood just got red and burned. And then it changed to ashes. But the ashes are a lot smaller than the wood. How come?

M: It could be that the wood turned into something else that went up and out the chimney, but you couldn't see it. After all, you did say that the wood burns *up*!

D: Something I can't see? If I couldn't see it then it would be invisible!

M: Yes, why not? What do you know that's invisible?

D: Air. Air is invisible.

M: What else?

D: I don't know.

M: Sure you do. What about water?

172

D: I can see water. It's not invisible.

M: Not when it evaporates.

D: That's true. When the water bits get farther apart and rise up into the air they become invisible. When wood burns, is it like water evaporating?

M: No, because wood isn't water. But it can change into water.

D: It can?

M: And into other invisible things too, when it burns!

D: What other invisible things?

M: An invisible gas that goes out the chimney with the water vapor.

D: The wood changes to invisible things that go out the chimney then?

M: Yes. And to ashes too. It changes to invisible gases, water vapor, and ashes.

D: Well, it must make a lot of water vapor and gases because the ashes are so light. All the rest of the wood, except for the ashes, changed to vapor and gases and went out the chimney then.

M: That's true

D: But it's not like evaporation of water?

M: No, it isn't, because water vapor can condense back to liquid water. The water vapor, gases, and ashes from burning wood can't be changed back into logs.

D: You're right, they can't.

M: Water doesn't change to a new thing when it evaporates. It just changes from liquid water to gaseous water. And it can condense back from a gas to a liquid. That's called a physical change. Like melting or boiling. No new things are formed.

D: What's it called when wood changes to the new things—the ashes, water vapor, and gases?

M: It's called a chemical change or a chemical reaction.

D: What's a chemical?

M: Just about everything is a chemical. Wood, water, metal, food—even air. All of those things are chemicals.

D: Even me? Am I a chemical?

M: Well, yes. You're a mixture of lots of chemicals. And so is food. And when you eat food it undergoes a lot of different changes and it turns into you. It's how you grow.

D: What has that got to do with burning logs?

M: I was just explaining about chemical reactions. When chemicals change from one kind to another, it's called a chemical change. A log burning is an example of a chemical change. And food changing into you is another example.

D: And that's different from water freezing or evaporating?

M: Yes, because when water freezes you still have the same thing. Liquid water, ice, and gaseous water vapor are all one thing—water. And they can go back and forth from solid to liquid to gas. Those are all physical changes.

D: I can't change back into the food I ate, so food turning into me must be a chemical change!

M: That's right. Chemical changes can't easily go back and forth. A log can't unburn and you can't uneat and make back the food you ate yesterday.

D: Are there only two chemical changes, burning things and eating things?

M: No, there are thousands and thousands of different chemical changes. Two common ones we see are things growing, which happens relatively slowly, and things burning, which happens more rapidly.

D: What are some other chemical changes?

M: Add vinegar to some baking soda in a glass and watch what happens.

[They go to the kitchen and put two teaspoons of baking soda in a glass. Then D. pours in some vinegar.]

D: Wow! It gets all foamy and bubbly. What happened?

M: The vinegar and the baking soda change into new things. And one of the new things is a gas which bubbles off. We say the vinegar *reacted* with the baking soda to make the new things. It's a chemical change.

D: So in a chemical change things have to react with each other to make new things?

M: In most cases that's how it happens, though sometimes things will change all by themselves if you heat them.

D: What about the logs in the fire. Did they change all by themselves?

M: No, they reacted with oxygen, an invisible gas in the air.

D: That would mean that they wouldn't burn if there were no air.

M: That's true. They wouldn't.

D: Boy, sometimes it's hard to see a chemical change happen. How do you know that a chemical change is happening.

M: There are things you can look for.

D: What things?

M: If a gas or heat comes off, or if something changes color, or if a solid forms in a clear solution, then a chemical change might be occurring.

D: Can we do some more chemical changes?

M: We do them all the time. The burning candles at dinner last night were changing from candle wax to water vapor and invisible gases. The leaves we burned in the trash barrel were doing the same thing. Those were chemical changes.

D: What else?

M: The reaction of metal with oxygen in the air to make rust is a chemical change. Your old bike fender has rust spots all over it. Each spot is where a chemical change took place.

D: But I mean like the baking soda and vinegar chemical change. Can we do another one in a glass like that?

M: Ok. Let's take some of this cabbage juice from the purple cabbage I'm boiling and put it in a glass.

[M. pours hot liquid from boiling purple cabbage into a glass and lets it cool for a few minutes.]

D: What do I do?

M: Divide the juice up into four separate portions in four glasses.

D: Ok, what next?

M: Add some lemon juice to one, leave one alone, add some ammonia cleaner to the third, and baking soda to the last one. Watch what happens.

[Adds juice, ammonia, and baking soda as noted]

D: They make different colors! The lemon juice turns it pink and the ammonia turns it green. The baking soda turns it blue! And the one with nothing is still purple. What are the colors from?

M: They're from chemical reactions. The lemon juice has chemicals in it that react with the purple chemicals in the cabbage juice to change it to something new. Something that is pink!

D: And the ammonia has chemicals in it that react with the cabbage juice to make a new thing which is green?

M: Yes, that's what happened. That's another chemical change.

D: They are very pretty.

M: Chemical changes are often very pretty. Fireworks on the Fourth of July are also chemical changes. They produce a lot of heat and light as well as colors. Heat and light are also indications of a chemical reaction, just like color changes.

D: I like chemical changes better than physical changes. They're a lot more fun than watching water evaporate, boil, or freeze.

M: Well, they often are more colorful. But I think what you like is the speed with which some of them occur. Your rusting bike in the back yard is an example of a very slow chemical change and you wouldn't enjoy sitting in a chair and watching it happen. It takes weeks.

D: That's true. I want to see the changes happen fast. Like fireworks, burning logs, vinegar foaming, and cabbage colors.

M: Maybe we should buy you a chemistry set so you could try lots of different chemical changes.

D: Yes, let's buy one. Let's do it this afternoon. Where do they sell them?

M: You'll let me do your chemical changes with you, won't you?

D: Yes, Mommy, I will. I promise. Where do they sell them?

M: At the hobby store in the mall I think.

D: Can we get an ice cream sundae at the mall too?

M: I suppose we could.

D: You said when I eat things and they change into me, that's a chemical reaction.

M: I did, yes.

D: Then changing a chocolate sundae into me will be the first chemical reaction I do this afternoon!

Reacting—A Description

All the changes described in Chapters 1 through 8 are physical changes. In a physical change, a substance retains its identity. It's still the same thing, but in a different form. For example, when water freezes it's still water, but in a different form or state. It just changes from a liquid to a solid. And we can melt it back to a liquid. Similarly, when water boils and changes to vapor, it's still water. When we mix things like sand and salt, the sand and salt are still there. They're just mixed together. We could separate them if we wanted to spend the time doing it. And when we dissolve salt or sugar in water they're also still there. We can get them back by evaporating off the water.

Chemical changes are different than physical changes. A chemical change *transforms a substance into something completely different.* As we noted above, when liquid water is cooled below its freezing point it undergoes a physical change and becomes ice. But it can easily melt back to liquid water when the temperature is raised from below freezing to above freezing. When a substance undergoes a chemical change to something new it can't be made to go back to the original substance simply by changing the temperature.

When a chemical change occurs this means that substances *react* or combine with each other to form new substances. These combinations are called *reactions.* An example of a reaction is the burning of a log. When a log is heated it doesn't melt. If the temperature is high enough the wood reacts with the oxygen in the air to form new solids and gases (ashes, water vapor, and carbon dioxide gas). The common term for this particular chemical reaction is burning. When a log burns, it is undergoing a chemical change to something new. We can write a *chemical equation* to express how this happens:

wood + oxygen -> ashes + water vapor + carbon dioxide
gas

The "+" signs in the equation mean *"and."* The little arrow means *"goes to."* So we can read the equation like this: logs *and* oxygen *go to* ashes *and* water vapor *and* carbon dioxide gas. This is an example of a chemical change. Wood and oxygen have changed to something new and different. The chemical equation is a shorthand way of expressing the change. It is irreversible. You can't combine ashes, water vapor, and carbon dioxide in the fireplace and get logs back. The chemical change also gives off heat and light. Not all chemical reactions do this, but many do.

There are many different kinds of chemical changes. Compounds (Chapter 5) can react with each other to form new and different compounds. Elements can react to form compounds. Elements can react with compounds to form new compounds. Compounds can decompose into elements. All of these are chemical changes. Some examples are:

compounds + compounds -> new compounds

baking soda + vinegar -> sodium acetate + carbon dioxide gas + water

element + element -> compound

iron + oxygen -> iron oxide (rust)

copper + sulfur -> copper sulfide

elements + compounds -> new compounds

oxygen + wood -> water + carbon dioxide gas + ash

Let's consider the common chemical change called rusting. A piece of the element iron, like any substance, is composed of a very large number of very tiny bits. These iron bits are stacked very closely together in the piece of solid iron. The element oxygen is also composed of tiny bits. These are different than the iron bits. They don't weigh the same and they are not the same size. At room temperature they are in the gaseous state and thus the oxygen bits are much farther apart from each other than the bits in iron. That's why we can't see oxygen gas. The air around us has a lot of oxygen in it.

When the two elements—oxygen gas and iron metal—react with each other in a chemical change to form rust, the iron bits and oxygen bits become attached to each other, forming small bits of a new compound called iron oxide. This is commonly known as rust. While iron is a silvery-gray metal and oxygen is a colorless gas, iron oxide is a reddish-brown solid.

The chemical changes which occur in living things are usually much more complex than those which involve non-living things. For example, plants absorb carbon dioxide from the air and water from the soil. Under the influence of sunlight these are converted into cellulose and sugars in the plant. These are very complicated chemical changes.

When we eat, drink, and breathe in oxygen from the air, very complex chemical changes occur in our bodies which convert the food, water, and oxygen into the chemicals from which we are made.

Reacting

| substance A and B before reaction | substance A and B reacting to form AB | substance A and B reacting to form AB | completely formed new substance AB |

Experiments

YOU WILL NEED:
a glass
bottle
pot
10 clear plastic
    cups
balloon
baking soda
vinegar
purple cabbage
boiling water

lemon juice
pickle juice
salt
sugar
hamburger
    or chicken
various food-type
    liquids
various other
    solids

Experiments in reacting are quite different from all the other experiments you have been doing in this book. They involve *chemical changes*. All the other changes you have been reading and writing about, and experimenting with, have been physical changes. No new things are created in a physical change. If water evaporates to a vapor, it can be condensed again back to a liquid. Whether you have liquid or vapor, you still have the same thing—water. Evaporation and condensation are simple physical changes. *If you change a substance chemically you make something new.* You can't easily get the original substance back just by changing the temperature. Now let's begin with our first chemical change.

Add a half a teaspoon of baking soda to a glass. Write a detailed description of it, listing all its properties (color, odor, state—solid, liquid, or gas). Fill another glass about a third full of vinegar and list all its properties (color, odor, state—solid, liquid, or gas). Pour the vinegar into the glass containing the baking soda. Write a description of what you see happening. Write a word equation for what you see. Use the "+" symbol for the word "and." Use the arrow symbol "->" for the words "goes to." What new things can you see that are formed from the baking soda and vinegar?

 Repeat the same experiment, but this time put the vinegar in a bottle. Put the baking soda in a balloon over the top of the bottle, but don't let it fall in the vinegar until you have connected the balloon tightly (see picture below).

BAKING SODA
IN BALLOON
OVER BOTTLE

VINEGAR IN BOTTLE

Then lift up the balloon and let the baking soda fall in. What happens? Can you explain what might be happening?

 With your parent's help, add finely shredded purple cabbage to a pot of boiling water and stir it with a spoon for 15 minutes. Let the mixture stand overnight and then pour off the purple solution, in portions, into 10 clear plastic cups. Add drops of different liquids to the 10 portions of purple solution. Try vinegar, lemon juice, pickle juice, a solution of baking soda in water, as well as other food-type liquids from the kitchen. You could also try adding a bit of salt, sugar, or other solids. What do you see? Can you explain what might be happening?

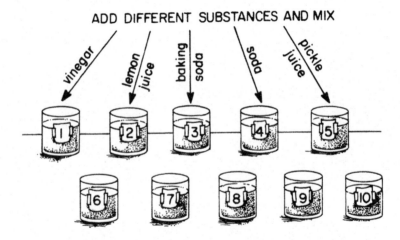

ADD DIFFERENT SUBSTANCES AND MIX

10 PORTIONS OF PURPLE CABBAGE EXTRACT

 The next time your mom or dad cooks hamburger or chicken for dinner write down a detailed description of the meat before it is cooked. Carefully record all its properties (odor, color, texture, hardness, etc.). After it's cooked, carefully observe the meat and again record all of its properties. What differences are there in the meat before and after it is cooked? What might have happened to make the changes occur? What other foods change when you cook them? Make a list. What might make cake batter rise up when it is baked in the oven (think about your bottle experiment above)?

 Have your mom or dad get you a chemistry set from the hobby store. Carefully read the manual that comes with the set, and **with your parent's help,** try to do some of the chemical reactions described in the manual. Keep a careful record of the properties of the reactants and products in each reaction and try to write a chemical word equation for the changes that occur. You need not use formulas.

Questions to Write and Draw

 What is a chemical reaction? Give an example and write a description. What is a chemical equation? What do the "->" and "+" symbols mean in a chemical equation?

 Explain how physical change is different from chemical change. List three examples of physical changes and three examples of chemical changes.

 Get a bag of green and red gumdrops (other colors are fine if you can't find red and green, but substitute other letters for R and G in the experiment below). Let green gumdrops represent small bits of substance G and red gumdrops represent small bits of substance R. Using toothpicks, show the "reaction" of G with R to give a new compound, GR, as in the following equation:

$$G \ + \ R \ -> \ GR$$

The toothpick serves as a bond from G to R. Can you write the chemical equation for the formation of a new compound of formula GR_2 from two red gumdrops and one green gumdrop? Can you use toothpicks and gumdrops to make the new compound GR_2? Can you write equations and make new compounds, using toothpicks, for G_2R and G_2R_3?

 In doing the above, remember that in a compound (where gumdrops are held together with toothpicks) the number of red and green gumdrops in the compound is designated by subscripts after each symbol. For example, in G_2R_3 there are two green gumdrops and three red ones. Here is the equation for formation of G_2R_3 from G and R:

$$2\,G \ + \ 3\,R \ -> \ G_2R_3$$

reactants   product

The number of gumdrops reacting (on the left side of the equation) is designated by a number (called a coefficient) in front of the symbol. For example, to form G_2R_3 you must have 2 G's and 3 R's. Remember, a subscript is a number that follows a symbol and is a little below it, whereas a coefficient is in front of a symbol and on the same line as the symbol.

 Using different colors, invent some new "reactions" with different numbers of gumdrops. After you are done you can eat the reactants and products. Make sure you take all the toothpicks out first!

 Can you make a list of indications that a chemical reaction is occurring?

 Draw a picture of a piece of wood burning. Under the picture write a word equation for the reaction. What things are in your word equation that *aren't* in the picture? *(Hint: they are invisible gases and vapors).* If something is in your word equation but isn't in the picture, how did you know it was in the equation? What evidence is there that it is there?

For Parents and Teachers

Getting Started

Chemical changes are exciting for children and there are many simple ones you can use to get started. Before you begin, it is important to discuss the difference between physical change and chemical change. If you have been using this book in a sequential fashion, by this time you have investigated many different kinds of physical change. Start by reviewing the vaporization of water and contrasting it with a burning match.

Drop a little water on a very hot hot plate. Then strike a match and let it burn. Ask children to call out what they see happening in these two changes. As they do, put their comments in separate lists on the blackboard, a transparency, or a piece of paper. The lists will be similar to the following:

water drops on hot plate	*burning match*
sizzles	hisses
drops move around	makes light
water changes to vapor (gas)	makes smoke and gases
water disappears	gets hot
steams	match turns black
etc.	etc.

Emphasize the differences between these two changes. Ask the children if there is any way you could get the water back. They may remember the process of condensation. If not, you could condense the vapor back into liquid by holding a glass of ice water above the steam coming from the hotplate. The vapor will form a film of water on the surface of the cold glass. Recall for them the experiments in condensing that you did.

Ask if there is any way they could get the match back. Some creative children with good imaginations may make up fanciful ways of doing this, but you should point out the difficulties of really doing it. In fact, it cannot be done. The burning match is an irreversible change. The match is wood and the head of the match is made from several chemicals. When the wood and chemicals burn and change to carbon, smoke, and other products, they cannot be recovered and changed back into the match. This is a basic characteristic of many chemical changes. They go only one way, in contrast to physical changes which are easily reversed.

Make a list of observations on the blackboard, a transparency, or a piece of paper which are associated with a chemical change:

color change
heat given off
light given off
solid forms in a solution
gas evolves
noise results
solid dissolves

Some of these observations are similar to those which occur in a physical change. For example, a gas forms when water boils and a solid forms when it freezes. However, these changes occur under quite different circumstances than during a chemical change. The example of a burning match and vaporizing water drops illustrates this. *Again, a primary difference is that chemical change is usually irreversible.* The gases from the burning match cannot be converted back to the unburnt match. The gas (water vapor) from the boiling water drops could be condensed back into water if they touched a cold surface.

To begin the exploration of chemical change, give each child two small plastic cups, one a quarter full of vinegar and one containing a teaspoon of baking soda. After they have written down a description of each of these (appearance, odor, color, etc.), have them pour the vinegar into the baking soda. Make sure the glass is big enough so that the foam does not overflow. Try it first by yourself before you meet with the children! Have them draw a picture of what they see, and write a description of the process. They should do the same for the final mixture (appearance, odor, color, etc.). If you are working at home with your children, go over these lists with them, giving supporting comments. See if they wish to make any changes or revisions. If you are working with a larger group in school, you can have children get into groups of three and share their pictures and descriptions to see if they saw and wrote similar things. They can revise and add to their writing during these discussions.

After ten minutes have them get out of their groups and assemble as a group of the whole. They can volunteer their observations of the reaction of vinegar with baking soda to you by raising their hands. You should collect all these on the blackboard or transparency so that everyone can see what has been generated by the group. Focus on those observations characterizing a chemical change (gas forms, solid dissolves, noise is heard). Ask them if the chemical change could be reversed. "Could the gas that forms and the clear solution that results be changed back into vinegar and baking soda?" The answer may not be obvious to them, and the class could discuss this question for a bit. You might want to vary the experiment by doing it in a soda bottle which you can cover with a balloon to trap the gas (see the Experiment section).

Write the chemical equation in words:

vinegar + baking soda -> gas + solution

A more detailed chemical version of this equation is as follows:

a solution of **acetic acid** *in water*	**sodium bicarbonate,** *a white solid*	->	**carbon dioxide,** *a gas bubbling up*	+ **water** +	**sodium acetate,** *a white solid dissolved water*

REACTANTS	PRODUCTS

The acetic acid is actually a dilute solution of this substance in water (vinegar), and the sodium acetate is dissolved in the water at the end of the reaction. The carbon dioxide gas escapes as bubbles into the air in the room. This is the foam that bubbles up and subsides as the reaction proceeds. For the meanings of the formulas see Chapter 5 as well as the *Deeper Look* section below.

You may wish to do the cabbage juice experiment described in the dialogue as a demonstration for the whole class. To do this, you can chop up some purple cabbage in a blender, along with some hot water, and filter this through a coffee filter. You will need this purple juice, along with some lemon juice, baking soda solution, and clear ammonia cleaner (no dye). When lemon juice is added to the purple cabbage juice, or when the ammonia cleaner is added, chemical reactions take place in which new colored compounds form. The children can record their observations and write qualitative "chemical reactions" to express them:

cabbage juice + lemon juice -> new pink substance
    (purple)   (colorless)   (pink)

cabbage juice + ammonia cleaner -> new green substance
    (purple)   (colorless)   (green)

The colors may vary a bit depending on how acidic the lemon juice is and what kind of ammonia cleaner you use.

To demonstrate chemical change in terms of submicroscopic bits, you can take two containers of differently colored marshmallows or gumdrops. It doesn't really matter what color they are, but don't mix them up. These will represent the tiny bits of two different compounds or two different elements.

Chemical change can be represented by taking a toothpick and putting a different colored gumdrop on either end. This represents a new compound (see the Questions to Write and Draw section). A red gumdrop is different from a green gumdrop and each of these is different from a combination—a toothpick with a different color on each end. If you can't find appropriately colored gumdrops, two differently sized gumdrops will work just as well. You can "react" a large gumdrop with a small one (connect them together with a toothpick) to get a new substance, a small and large gumdrop connected together.

reactant 1 + reactant 2 -> product

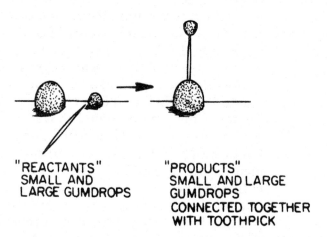

"REACTANTS"
SMALL AND
LARGE GUMDROPS

"PRODUCTS"
SMALL AND LARGE
GUMDROPS
CONNECTED TOGETHER
WITH TOOTHPICK

This gumdrop model of chemical change is not perfect. It might seem that taking the gumdrops off the toothpick (taking apart the new product) would be a model of the reverse "reaction" going back to the reactants, the single gumdrops. Most chemical reactions go in one direction much more readily than in the reverse direction, however.

A Deeper Look

Chemical change is more complicated than physical change. It is for this reason that *Where Puddles Go* has been mostly about physical change. The subtitle reflects this emphasis. Nevertheless, chemical change is even more important in explaining changes in the natural world. This chapter on *Reacting* is an introduction to the subject. The material in this section is really the very beginning of reaction chemistry as taught in middle and high school, though quantitative aspects of the subject are not dealt with here.

One of the most basic chemical changes is the reaction of two elements to give a compound. When the space shuttle is launched, the heat and flame results from the reaction of two elements, hydrogen and oxygen, to produce a compound, water. Many common elements react to form compounds. The reaction of iron with oxygen in the air to produce rust, iron oxide, is another example. Two other common elements, which can be purchased at the hardware store, are copper, in the form of wire, and sulfur, a common garden chemical.

If you take pieces of copper wire, mix them with half as much sulfur powder (by weight), and heat the mixture, it will react to give a silver gray solid. This solid is a new compound called copper sulfide. The chemical reaction is:

copper metal + sulfur –> copper sulfide
ELEMENTS   NEW COMPOUND

While you need not carry out this reaction, it is easily done in a laboratory by putting copper and sulfur in a test tube that is capped with a rubber balloon to keep the fumes of hot sulfur in. Heating with a Bunsen burner flame for about five minutes is sufficient to complete the reaction. For a detailed procedure see Experiment No. 22 in the Teacher Edition of *Chemical Activities*, by C. L. Borgford and L. R. Summerlin, An American Chemical Society publication, Washington D.C., 1988.

The representation of this change using chemical symbols is:

$$Cu + S \rightarrow CuS$$

The symbol for copper metal is Cu from the Latin *aes Cyprium,* literally, "metal of Cyprus." The symbol for sulfur is the first letter of the word in English. The compound, CuS, is completely different in character from either of the elemental reactants. It is a new substance with different properties (color, hardness, texture, etc.) than either element, copper or sulfur.

In the chemical equation, Cu can mean one copper atom (the tiny bit in the children's descriptive text) and the symbol S can mean one sulfur atom. The symbol CuS means a *formula unit* of the new compound copper sulfide containing one copper atom and one sulfur atom. The symbols Cu and S can also mean a *very large number* of copper atoms (large enough to see), *a very large but equal number* of sulfur atoms (also large enough to see) and *a very large but equal number* of copper sulfide formula units (also large enough to see).

Since a copper atom weighs about twice as much as a sulfur atom, and since the *very large number* referred to above is the same for the copper, the sulfur, and the copper sulfide, the weight of the visible pile of copper should be twice that of the weight of the visible pile of sulfur. If there is more copper than this, some will be left over at the end of the reaction. If there is less copper, sulfur will be left over at the end of the reaction.

The reaction between copper and sulfur is an example of a reaction between two elements to give a new compound. There are many reactions of this type. Classifying chemical change is, in large part, classifying different kinds of chemical reactions.

The symbols in chemical equations that represent chemical reactions are like words in sentences. There are the symbols for the substances, the arrow symbol, which means "goes to," as well as the + signs which mean "and."

In formulas, a subscript after a letter symbol indicates how many atoms of that particular type are in the formula unit or molecule. If that number is one, as in the case of copper sulfide, Cu_1S_1, generally it is left out, as in CuS. If it is an integer other than one, like the two in H_2O, it is not left out.

Glossary

absorb: The entry, into the body of a solid or liquid, of another substance with which it is in contact.

air: The invisible mixture of gases in the atmosphere, consisting of about seventy-eight percent nitrogen, twenty-one percent oxygen and one percent argon. Air also contains small amounts of carbon dioxide, variable amounts of water vapor, and very small amounts of other gases.

alcohol: A class of organic compound containing a hydrocarbon group attached to a hydroxyl group (water-like group). There are two common types of alcohol. Ethyl alcohol is the intoxicating, beverage alcohol. Isopropyl alcohol is commonly called rubbing alcohol. It is usually used externally as an aqueous solution to soothe, refresh, or lower body temperature.

aluminum: A silvery, light, metallic element. Aluminum, like most metals, is a good conductor of heat and electricity. In chemical combination it is the most abundant metal in the earth's crust.

amorphous solid: A solid which does not have a crystalline form. The molecules or ions in an amorphous solid have a random and nonrepetitive three-dimensional arrangement.

aqueous solution: A homogeneous mixture of two or more substances dissolved in water.

atom: The smallest part of an element that has the characteristics of that element. All the atoms of any one element are chemically identical. An atom is composed of even smaller particles called *protons, neutrons, and electrons* (see below). The protons and neutrons, which are much heavier than the electrons, are in the center of the atom—the atomic nucleus. The electrons exist outside the nucleus. The proton has a positive charge equal in magnitude to that of the electron. The neutron has no charge. In a neutral atom the number of electrons is the same as the number of protons, so there is no net charge. If electrons are lost from the atom, a positive ion results. If the atom gains electrons, a negative ion results.

baking soda: The chemical, sodium bicarbonate. It is a white solid, composed of sodium ions and bicarbonate ions, which is soluble in water.

binary mixture: A mixture containing only two components.

boil: The common term for vaporization of a liquid, usually water. When water is heated and brought to a boil, bubbles of water vapor are seen in the liquid.

boiling point: The temperature at which a liquid boils. The boiling point of water is 100 degrees centigrade or 212 degrees Fahrenheit at a pressure of one atmosphere (one atmosphere is defined as that air pressure which will hold up a 760 mm high column of mercury in a mercury barometer). At lower atmospheric pressures—atop a mountain for example—the boiling point is lower. At sea level the pressure is near one atmosphere.

burn: To undergo combustion. The common meaning refers to chemical reaction of an organic substance, like wood, with oxygen in the atmosphere to produce oxidation products like carbon dioxide, water, as well as heat, and light.

carbon: A nonmetallic element commonly found in nature as diamond or graphite, or as a component of coal. Chemically combined, carbon is the basic element of organic compounds.

carbon dioxide: A relatively heavy, colorless gas that is formed by the combustion of organic substances with oxygen. It is absorbed from the air by plants in photosynthesis and is converted into complex molecules like cellulose and sugars. It is also one of the end products of animal metabolism. A carbon dioxide molecule results from the chemical combination of one atom of carbon and two atoms of oxygen.

centigrade temperature scale: A temperature scale in which the interval between the freezing point and the boiling point of water is divided into one-hundred degrees, with zero representing the freezing point and one-hundred the boiling point. (From the Latin *centum* "hundred" + *gradus* "step, degree") The centigrade scale is also called the Celsius scale.

change of state: The transformation of one state of a single substance (solid, liquid, or gas) to another. Changes of state are reversible. The melting of ice to liquid water is an example of a change of state, as is the vaporization of liquid water to water vapor. Changes of state either require heat (as does melting) or give off heat (as does freezing).

charge: An excess or deficiency of electrons, small negative particles. An excess of electrons produces a *negative* charge whereas a deficiency of electrons produces a *positive* charge. Positive and negative charges can coexist on a single neutral species. Such species are called polar and contain a positive pole and a negative pole.

chemical change or *chemical combination:* The transformation of a substance, or substances, to new substances of a different kind. Chemical change contrasts with physical change in which a substance simply changes its form (solid to liquid, for example, or liquid to vapor). Chemical changes are usually irreversible. For example, the elements sodium and chlorine chemically combine to give the compound sodium chloride, table salt, an ionic compound (see *ion* below).

chemical formula: The representation of a substance by symbols denoting the amount and type of elements it contains. A formula shows the symbols for the elements combined in the substance, along with subscripts indicating how many atoms of each element are included. For example, the chemical formula of water is H_2O, indicating that two atoms of hydrogen and one atom of oxygen are in one molecule of water.

chemical property: The characteristics of a substance relating to the way in which it reacts with other substances. Chemical properties can only be observed in chemical reactions where changes in the identity of a substance occur.

chemical reaction: See chemical change.

chemicals: Any substance, either an element, a compound, or mixtures of these.

chemistry: The science that deals with the composition, structure, properties, and uses of substances, and the changes they undergo.

chloride ion: The negative species that results when a chlorine atom acquires an electron, a small negative particle. This acquisition commonly occurs during the chemical reaction of elemental chlorine. For example, a sodium atom can lose an electron to yield a positive sodium ion. This lost electron can be acquired by a chlorine atom to give the negative chloride ion. The resultant product is sodium chloride, an ionic compound (sodium + chlorine $->$ sodium chloride).

chlorine: A greenish-yellow, gaseous, nonmetallic chemical element which is extremely irritating and toxic. Chlorine is very reactive. It combines with sodium, a reactive metallic element, to yield sodium chloride (common table salt).

chromatography: Techniques which separate a mixture of substances, often of various colors, into pure components. There are many different kinds of chromatography. One common type is paper chromatography, where a liquid travels up a paper strip containing a spot of the mixture. The components of the mixture are separated out on the paper as the liquid passes by it.

cloud: A large collection of very small droplets of water suspended high in the atmosphere. When close to the ground this collection is often called a fog or mist.

coefficient: The number *preceding* the formula in a chemical equation indicating the amount of the substance taking part in the reaction. For example, in the following equation for the formation of water from hydrogen and oxygen, $2 H_2 + O_2 -> 2H_2O$, the number 2 which appears in front of H_2 and H_2O is a coefficient. It indicates that 2 hydrogen molecules react with one oxygen molecule to give 2 water molecules. When the coefficient is unity (one), as in the case of oxygen above, it is not shown. Coefficients are to be distinguished from subscripts, numbers written below and to the right of a symbol in a formula to indicate the number of atoms present in the formula. In the above example the small 2 between H and O in the formula for water indicates that a water molecule contains two hydrogens.

cold: A condition of relatively low temperature, or a temperature below normal.

compound: A substance composed of two or more elements chemically combined in a definite proportion by weight.

concentration: A measure of the quantity of substance dissolved in a solution.

conclusion: A final reasoned judgment made from observations (often of the results of experiments).

condensation: The process by which a vapor is changed to a liquid. Condensation is one example of a change of state.

condenser: Part of an apparatus used to change a vapor into a liquid. Often it will have a cold surface with which hot vapor comes into contact, cools, and condenses to the liquid. See *distillation.*

copper: A reddish, metallic element which is a very good conductor of heat and electricity.

crystal: A solid in which the molecules or ions have a characteristic, regular, and repeating three-dimensional arrangement. Single crystals often have external plane faces. For example, crystals of sodium chloride are cubes.

crystallization: The process of crystal formation. Crystallization can occur when a pure liquid is cooled to its freezing point. A pure substance can also crystallize from a concentrated solution if the temperature is lowered or if the solvent evaporates.

decomposition: The breakdown of a substance, through chemical change, into new substances.

dissolve: To go into solution. A solute (e.g., sugar) *dissolves* in a solvent (e.g., water) to give a solution.

distillation: A process in which a mixture of liquids is vaporized by heating, and then condensed by cooling; often used for purposes of purifying or separating liquids.

electrical force: an attractive influence (i.e., a pull) between two particles which results from their opposite charges. For example, a positively charged particle is attracted to a negatively charged particle (e.g., positive sodium ion is attracted to negative chloride ion). See *charge*.

electrolysis: The decomposition or chemical change of a compound, usually in the liquid state, caused by passing an electrical current through it. The current is carried through the liquid by positive and negatively charged particles (see *ions*). These particles may form the liquid, or they may be added to it as a solute. An example is the electrolysis of water containing the dissolved ionic compound sodium sulfate: $2 H_2O$ (liquid) $2->$ $2 H_2$ (gas) $+ O_2$ (gas). The current in the water is carried by the positive sodium ions and the negative sulfate ions. These do not appear in the equation because they are not changed during the electrolysis.

electron: A small, fundamental, negatively charged, subatomic particle. The electron exists outside the nucleus in an atom. It has a very small mass compared to the proton or neutron.

element: One of one-hundred and six fundamental forms of substance that cannot be separated into simpler substances. Elements contain only atoms of the same type. This is in contrast to molecules, which may contain more than one kind of atom.

element symbol: A single capital letter, or a set of two letters with the first capitalized, which represents one atom of an element or a large collection of atoms of an element. The letters are often derived from English, Latin, or Greek names. For example, H is the symbol for the element hydrogen, an English transliteration from the Greek words meaning "water former" (hydrogen forms water when it is burned in air). Au is the symbol for the element gold, from the Latin *aurum* "shining dawn". Br is the symbol for the element bromine, from the Greek *bromos* "bad smell". Other elements have been named to honor famous scientists, or the places where they were discovered, e.g., Es for Einsteinium and Cf for Californium. Ions and molecules can be symbolized by combining element symbols and placing subscripts (numbers) and superscripts (charges) adjacent to the combinations. See *molecule, ion, charge,* and *chemical formula.*

equation: A symbolic representation, using element, molecule and/or ion symbols, which represents a chemical change. The atom and molecule symbols in the equation are separated by "+" signs which mean "and". The products and reactants are separated by an arrow symbol "−>" which means "goes to." For example, the chemical change: "sodium and water go to sodium hydroxide and hydrogen" is represented as follows, $2\ Na + 2\ H_2O\ 2\ -> 2\ NaOH + H_2$. The chemical change: "copper and sulfur go to copper sulfide" is represented by $Cu + S\ -> CuS$.

evaporation: The change of a liquid to its vapor when molecules entering the vapor state do so only at the surface of the liquid. Evaporation is usually considered to occur well below the boiling point of the liquid. When a liquid changes into its vapor at the boiling point, this change of state is usually called vaporization.

experiment: An operation or procedure carried out under controlled conditions to test or help establish whether an hypothesis is true or false. In more specific chemical terms, the hypothesis might be that compound "X" would form from the reaction of "A" and "B". An experiment would be to mix "A" and "B" under different conditions to see if they do indeed react to form "X". Such an experiment would test the hypothesis.

extensive property: A quality or characteristic of a substance which depends on the amount of substance observed. Examples include mass, volume, or heat content. The heat contained in a pot of boiling water is much greater than the heat contained in a cup of boiling water.

Fahrenheit temperature scale: A temperature scale in which the interval between the freezing point and the boiling point of water is divided into 180 degrees, with 32 degrees representing the freezing point and 212 degrees the boiling point. The Fahrenheit temperature scale is commonly used in everyday discourse in the United States, whereas the Celsius or centigrade temperature scale (see above) is used in most laboratories and in Canada and Europe.

filtration: A procedure for separating a mixture of an insoluble solid from a liquid by means of some porous medium. For example, a mixture of sand and water can be separated by pouring it through a porous piece of paper like a coffee filter.

fluid: A substance which flows and conforms to the shape of its container. Both liquids and gases are fluids. Gases fill their container completely whereas liquids are flat on top where they do not touch it.

fog: A large collection of very small droplets of water in the lower atmosphere near the ground. See *cloud.*

fool's gold: Iron pyrite, a sulfide of iron (FeS_2). Although it looks like the element gold, fool's gold is not an element, but a compound which is much less dense and much harder than gold.

formula: A combination of element symbols written together with appropriate *subscripts,* representing a compound. Subscripts are numbers written below and to the right of an element symbol in a formula to indicate the number of atoms of that element present in the formula. The small 2 between H and O in the formula for water, H_2O, indicates that a water molecule contains two hydrogens atoms for each oxygen atom.

freezing: The process by which a substance changes from its liquid to its solid state. When liquid water changes to ice it freezes.

frost: A covering of very small crystals of ice, formed on a cold surface when it comes into contact with water vapor in the air.

gas: That state of a substance in which the molecules are very far apart from each other and travel relatively long distances before colliding with other molecules. A gas has no definite shape, but fills the container which holds it. Unlike liquids and solids, gases are easily compressed and will occupy smaller volumes at higher pressures. Another term for gas is vapor.

glucose: A sugar found in honey, fruits, and blood. It is composed of the elements carbon, hydrogen, and oxygen in the ratios indicated by the subscripts in its formula, $C_6H_{12}O_6$. A common name for glucose is dextrose.

gram: A metric unit of mass equal to 1/1000 of a kilogram. A cubic centimeter of water at its maximum density has a mass of about 1 gram. One ounce is about 28.3 grams.

graph: A diagram that represents change in one variable factor on one axis of the diagram, and compares it with the change of another variable on the other axis. A graph of volume vs. temperature of a gas is a curved line which shows the volume increasing as the temperature increases.

heat: That form of energy associated with molecular or atomic motion. It is the energy transferred between objects that are at different temperatures. When flowing into a substance this energy causes the temperature to increase. In addition to causing a temperature increase, inward heat flow can cause a solid to melt, a liquid to vaporize, a gas to expand, and substances to undergo chemical changes. When flowing out of a substance, the heat loss causes the temperature of that substance to decrease. Under these conditions, in addition to decreasing in temperature, outward heat flow can cause a gas to decrease in volume and eventually condense, and a liquid to freeze.

heterogeneous mixture: A mixture in which the individual components remain physically separate. It does not have the same composition throughout. Heterogeneous mixtures of different compositions have different properties. Often the separate components in a heterogeneous mixture can be seen with the naked eye, but a microscope is sometimes needed. Granite is a heterogeneous mixture. A mixture of salt and sand is also a heterogeneous mixture. Such mixtures can be separated by physical means.

homogeneous mixture: A mixture in which the composition and appearance of the mixture are uniform throughout. No separate components can be seen, even with a microscope.

Homogeneous mixtures of different compositions, like heterogeneous mixtures, may have different properties and can be separated into their components by physical means (chemical changes are not necessary). Air is an example of a homogeneous mixture (of nitrogen and oxygen).

hot: A condition of relatively high temperature, or a temperature above normal.

humidity: The amount of water vapor in the air. The relative humidity is the ratio of the amount of water vapor actually present to the greatest amount possible at the same temperature.

hydrogen: A colorless, odorless, highly flammable, gaseous element. Hydrogen is the simplest and lightest of all the elements. It burns in air (reacting with oxygen) to produce water.

hypothesis: An unverified explanation of an observation that needs confirmation by further observations and/or experiments. A tentative explanation.

ice: The solid state of water.

insoluble: Incapable of being dissolved in a liquid or solvent, or soluble only to a very slight degree.

intensive property: A quality or characteristic of a substance which is independent of the amount of substance observed. Examples include density and temperature. The temperature of a pot of boiling water is the same as a cup of boiling water (one-hundred degrees centigrade).

iodine: A purple-black, nonmetallic, crystalline, solid element found chemically combined in seawater and seaweeds. The common antiseptic "iodine" found in drug stores is actually a solution of elemental iodine in alcohol, called a tincture.

ion: A single atom or a group of atoms that has acquired a negative charge by gaining electrons or a positive charge by losing electrons. An atom of sodium, Na, which has lost an electron, results in the positive sodium ion, Na^+. An atom of chlorine, Cl, which has acquired an electron, results in the negative chloride ion Cl^-. Positive ions are called cations.

Negative ions are called anions. Table salt, sodium chloride, formed from sodium ion and chloride ion, is an ionic compound with the formula $Na^{+1}Cl^{-1}$ or $NaCl$.

irreversible change: A change which goes only in one direction. Many chemical changes are irreversible. Burning wood is an example of a chemical change. To be distinguished from a *reversible change* (see below).

kinetic energy: That kind of energy associated with movement. The greater the velocity or speed of a moving molecule or atom, the greater its kinetic energy.

liquid: That state of a substance in which the molecules are relatively close to each other, but are not held in rigid positions. They are free to move about throughout the liquid. While a liquid does have a definite volume, it has no definite shape, but instead takes the shape of the container which holds it. Only the top of the liquid, where it does not touch the container, is flat.

magnetic force: An attractive influence (i.e., a pull) between two poles of a magnet, or between one pole of a magnet and certain magnetic substances like iron.

melting: The process by which a substance changes from its solid to its liquid state. When ice changes to liquid water it melts.

melting point: The temperature at which a substance changes from the solid to the liquid state. This is the same temperature at which a substance freezes from the liquid to the solid state, the freezing point. Though the melting and freezing points are identical, the latter is thought of as a property of the liquid and the former, a property of the solid. The difference between melting and freezing is simply the direction of heat flow. In melting, heat flows into the substance. In freezing it flows out.

metals: Elements that are lustrous, good conductors of heat and electricity, and which are ductile and malleable (easily hammered into a thin film or easily shaped by rollers and other pressure devices). Metals are listed on the left and in the middle of the periodic table of the elements. They readily react with nonmetals, losing electrons to form positive ions, while the nonmetals gain electrons to form negative ions. These positive and negative ions are the constitutents of the ionic compounds formed when metals react with nonmetals.

mixture: Two or more substances (elements or compounds) that are mixed together but not chemically combined. Substances in a mixture exist in no specific proportion to each other, and the composition of the mixture may vary. The substances in a mixture may be separated by physical means.

molecule: A chemically combined group of two or more like or unlike atoms. A water molecule contains two hydrogen atoms chemically combined with one oxygen atom. A molecule can be represented by a formula. For example, a water molecule is H_2O. A glucose molecule (blood sugar) is $C_6H_{12}O_6$. The subscripts represent the number of the particular atoms in the molecule to the upper left of the subscript. A water molecule contains two hydrogen atoms and only one oxygen atom. A glucose molecule contains six carbon atoms, twelve hydrogen atoms, and six oxygen atoms. H_2 is an example of a molecule which contains only one kind of atom.

neutron: A small, fundamental, neutral, subatomic particle which exists, along with protons, in the nucleus of an atom. It is very massive compared to the mass of an electron, but very nearly equal in mass to the proton.

nonmetal: Elements located in the upper right part of the periodic table. They are not good conductors of electricity or heat. They readily react with metals, gaining electrons to form negative ions.

nonpolar: A substance composed of molecules that do not have a separation of charge, i.e., there are no positive or negative poles (see *polar* below). Gasoline and turpentine are examples of nonpolar substances.

oil: A liquid which does not dissolve in water, but is soluble in hydrocarbon liquids like gasoline and turpentine. Two common types of oils are those derived from petroleum, like motor oil, and those derived from plants, like corn oil, peanut oil, and safflower oil. Plant-derived oils are edible foods which break down when they are digested. Petroleum-derived oils are not edible. Fats have a chemical structure similar to plant derived oils, but they are solids rather than liquids.

oxygen: A colorless, odorless, chemically reactive, gaseous element that comprises about 21 percent of the atmosphere. It is also the major component of water by weight. Oxygen readily combines chemically with all the other elements, except for some of the noble gases (helium, neon, and argon). Oxygen is the gas absorbed by animals when they breathe and is essential to life processes. It is also the gas which combines with substances when they undergo combustion. Reactions involving oxygen are often called oxidations.

periodic table: An arrangement of the elements into a table according to their chemical properties.

petri dish: A small shallow dish made of relatively thin glass. It comes with a loose cover and is useful for keeping substances dust free. Its primary use is for growing bacteria, but it has many other uses as well.

phase: Another term for *state.* There are three fundamental phases of matter: solid, liquid, and gas. The word comes from the Greek *phasis* "appearance of a star, phase of the moon."

physical change: The change of state of a substance from one phase to another. See *change of state* above.

physical property: The characteristics of a substance relating to the way it appears or exists, i.e., its color, weight, density, hardness, melting point, boiling point, etc. Physical properties can be measured or observed without changing the composition and identity of a substance. To be distinguished from *chemical property* (see above).

polar: The property of a substance caused by its having a positive or partial positive charge on one part of a molecule, and a negative or partial negative charge on another part of the same molecule. When positive and negative charges coexist on a single molecule the substance is called polar. Its molecules contain a positive pole and a negative pole. Polar substances are attracted to one another and are repelled by *nonpolar* substances. Water and alcohol are examples of polar substances.

product: The substance(s) formed from reactants during a chemical change.

proton: A small, fundamental, positively charged, subatomic particle that exists, along with neutrons, in the nucleus of an atom. It is very massive compared to the mass of an electron, but equal in mass to the neutron.

pure: The common meaning is uncontaminated. The chemical meaning is of a single substance, not mixed with any other substances, e.g., pure gold or pure salt. There are two kinds of pure substances, elements and compounds. Gold is a pure element. Salt (sodium chloride) is a pure compound. A mixture of elements, of elements and compounds, or of compounds is not pure.

quartz: A form of silica, a compound of silicon and oxygen, the formula for which is SiO_2. Quartz is often found as colorless, transparent, hexagonal-shaped crystals. It has a very high melting point (seventeen hundred degrees centigrade) and does not conduct electricity. Quartz is only one form of silica. There are more than a dozen forms altogether.

reactant: The substance(s) from which products form during a chemical change.

result: The consequence of a process or action. In chemistry, the products of a possible chemical change might *result* or *not result* if the reactants are heated under certain conditions. On the basis of observing the *results* of this mixing and heating, *conclusions* (see above) can be made: the reactants will or won't react to give products under the given conditions.

reversible change: That type of change which can be made to go in the opposite direction. Physical changes are reversible. Melting ice to water can be reversed by freezing water to ice. To be distinguished from *irreversible change* (see above).

rock candy: Table sugar, sucrose, crystallized into large massive crystals.

rock salt: Table salt, sodium chloride, crystallized into large crystals.

rusting: The reaction of iron with oxygen in the air to give iron oxide (ferric oxide), rust. Rust is a reddish-orange, brittle coating that appears on the surface of unprotected iron when it is exposed to moist air.

salt: The general chemical term refers to ionic compounds formed between positive ions and negative ions. The common meaning is sodium chloride, table salt, (NaCl), a specific example of the general chemical class. Table salt is composed of positive sodium ions, Na^+, and negative chloride ions, Cl^-.

scientific method: A sequence of actions which includes making hypotheses, doing experiments, observing results, drawing conclusions, deriving explanations, and confirming or disproving the original hypotheses. In practice it is really much more complex than this simple idealized sequence.

seed crystal: A small crystal of a substance added to a concentrated solution of that substance in a solvent in order to promote crystallization.

separation: The isolation of the components of a mixture into pure substances.

separatory funnel: A conical funnel with a valve (stopcock) at the bottom, used to separate two liquids of different density which do not dissolve in each other. The more dense liquid at the bottom of the funnel is drained off and the valve is shut before the less dense liquid can escape.

sleet: Frozen rain.

snow: Small hexagonal-shaped crystals of water formed directly from water vapor in the atmosphere.

sodium: A reactive, shiny, lustrous, metallic element which is a very good conductor of electricity. Sodium is soft, easily shaped, and has a very low melting point (eighty-three degrees centigrade). It is so reactive that it quickly combines with moisture in the air and becomes covered with a thin layer of sodium hydroxide (a strong caustic substance). For this reason, it is stored under kerosene or other unreactive hydrocarbon-like organic liquids. It should be distinguished from its compound sodium chloride, since many food product labels list sodium content. Those labels are referring to sodium chloride, not elemental sodium metal.

sodium ion: The positive ion that results when an elemental sodium atom loses an electron, a small negative particle. This commonly occurs during the chemical reaction of sodium (see *chloride ion*).

solder: A low melting mixture of the metals lead and tin, which when melted and then solidified, is used to join metal surfaces.

solid: That state of a substance in which the molecules or ions are packed very closely to each other in regular rigid arrays. The molecules or ions do not move freely about in the solid, but remain fixed in place. A solid has a specific volume and shape, and is not compressible.

solubility: The degree to which a substance dissolves in a solvent. Salt and sugar are very soluble in water. Sand is not.

soluble: Capable of being dissolved in a solvent.

solute: That part of a solution which is dissolved in the solvent.

solution: A uniform, homogeneous, mixture of substances, often a liquid, containing a completely dissolved substance.

solvent: Usually a liquid substance which dissolves one or more other substances (solutes).

state: Another term for *phase.* There are three fundamental states of matter: solid, liquid, and gas.

steam: A collection of very small droplets of water which briefly appear above the water surface when it is brought to its boiling point. These quickly dissipate into invisible water vapor.

sublimation: The process by which a substance changes directly from the solid state to the gaseous state without going through the liquid state. Two common substances which do this are the compound carbon dioxide ("dry ice") and the element iodine.

subscript: The small number which appears below and to the right of a symbol in a formula to indicate the number of atoms present in the formula. For example, in the formula for water, H_2O, the small 2 between H and O in the formula indicates that a water molecule contains two hydrogens for each oxygen. In the formula for hydrogen gas, H_2, the small 2 after the letter H indicates that there are two hydrogen atoms in a hydrogen molecule.

sucrose: See *sugar* below.

sugar: The general term refers to a class of water soluble, white, crystalline compounds of varying sweetness. They are called carbohydrates, and they contain the elements carbon, hydrogen, and oxygen. A common meaning for the term sugar is table sugar, or sucrose. Sucrose is obtained from sugar cane or sugar beets, and is a nutritionally important source of dietary carbohydrate and a sweetener. The other common sugars are glucose and fructose.

sulfur: A yellow, nonmetallic element, which occurs in nature, both in its elemental and its chemically combined forms. It does not conduct electricity. There are a variety of forms of elemental sulfur. One of the most common is yellow crystals.

superscript: A small symbol (usually a "+" or a "−" and a number) to the upper right of an element symbol or formula symbol. It usually represents a charge on the species. For example, Na^+ means that the sodium ion has one positive charge. Mg^{+2} means that the magnesium ion has two positive charges. Sometimes the number is written before the charge as in Mg^{2+}.

superheat: Heating a liquid beyond its boiling point without converting it to its vapor. This can occur when there are no surfaces upon which bubbles of vapor can easily form. Superheated liquids can often spontaneously boil very rapidly. To avoid superheating, small porous chunks of porcelain or other materials are often added to liquids which are to be vaporized. These provide surfaces upon which bubbles of vapor can form.

suspension: The state of a substance when it is mixed with a liquid and does not dissolve, but floats throughout the mixture or partially sinks to the bottom.

syrup: A very concentrated solution of sugar or sugars in water.

table salt: Sodium chloride, a white, crystalline, ionic compound formed from the elements sodium and chlorine. The formula for sodium chloride is NaCl.

temperature: A measure of the intensity of *heat* (see above), usually done with a thermometer. The general meaning of the term is the degree of "hotness" of an object. If two objects with different temperatures are brought into contact, the warmer object becomes colder (its temperature drops) and the colder object becomes warmer (its temperature increases) until both reach the same temperature.

thermometer: A device used to measure temperature which contains a small column of liquid in a thin capillary bore in a glass tube. As the temperature increases, the liquid in the capillary expands and increases its length in the liquid column. By placing marks on the outside of the tube a temperature scale is created.

unit: A definite quantity agreed upon as a standard of measurement. As an example, everyday units for mass and length are the pound and foot. In scientific laboratories, the metric system of units is used. Common metric units for weight and length are the gram and the centimeter.

vapor: See *gas* above.

vaporization: The process by which a liquid is converted to its gaseous state. Similar to boiling (see *boil* above).

vinegar: A sour, acidic substance obtained by the fermentation of cider and wine. Chemically, it is a dilute solution of acetic acid in water.

water: A clear, liquid compound (at room temperature) containing the elements hydrogen and oxygen. The formula for water is H_2O.

water vapor: The gaseous form of water.

Index

CPSIA information can be obtained
at www.ICGtesting.com
Printed in the USA
BVOW11s0735200717
489689BV00004B/37/P